**TEACHER'S PET PUBLICATIONS**

LITPLAN TEACHER PACK
for
Bless Me, Ultima
based on the book by
Rudolfo Anaya

Written by
Barbara M. Linde, MA Ed.

© 1995 Teacher's Pet Publications
All Rights Reserved

This **LitPlan** on Rudolfo Anaya's **Bless Me Ultima**
has been brought to you by Teacher's Pet Publications, Inc.

Copyright Teacher's Pet Publications 1995
11504 Hammock Point
Berlin MD 21811

Only the student materials in this unit plan may be
reproduced. Pages such as worksheets and study
guides may be reproduced for use in the purchaser's
classroom. For any additional copyright questions,
contact Teacher's Pet Publications.

www.tpet.com

TABLE OF CONTENTS - *Bless Me, Ultima*

Introduction	7
Unit Objectives	9
Unit Outline	10
Reading Assignment Sheet	11
Study Questions	15
Quiz/Study Questions (Multiple Choice)	29
Pre-Reading Vocabulary Worksheets	49
Lesson One (Introductory Lesson)	71
Nonfiction Assignment Sheet	75
Project Storyteller	78
Oral Reading Evaluation Form	80
Writing Assignment 1	83
Writing Evaluation Form	84
Writing Assignment 2	87
Extra Writing Assignments/Discussion ?s	91
Writing Assignment 3	99
Vocabulary Review Activities	100
Unit Review Activities	101
Unit Tests	107
Unit Resource Materials	143
Vocabulary Resource Materials	157

A FEW NOTES ABOUT THE AUTHOR
RUDOLFO ANAYA

ANAYA, Rudolfo (1937-). Rudolfo Anaya is one of the most widely read modern Mexican-American writers. He is best known for *Bless Me Ultima*, his first novel and winner of the Premio Quinto Sol, a national Chicano literary award.

Rudolfo Alfonso Anaya was born on October 30, 1937, in Pastura, New Mexico. His father, Martín, was a laborer. His mother was Rafaelita Mares Anaya. Anaya is married to Patricia Lawless, a counselor, and lives in Albuquerque, New Mexico.

Anaya received a BA in English from the University of New Mexico in 1963, and a MA in English in 1968. He also received an MA in guidance and counseling from the same university in 1972.

In addition to writing, Rudolfo Anaya has taught at the University of New Mexico, Albuquerque, since 1974. He became a full professor in 1988. He has also lectured at la Universidad Anahuac in Mexico City, Mexico, Yale, the University of Michigan, Michigan State University, the University of California at Los Angeles, the University of Indiana, and the University of Texas at Houston.

His professional memberships include the Modern Language Association, The American Association of University Professors, and the National Council of Teachers of English. He was the founder and first president of the Rio Grande Writers Association.

In 1971 Anaya received the Premio Quinto Sol literary award for *Bless Me, Ultima*. He received the University of New Mexico Mesa Chicana literary award in 1977, the New Mexico Governor's Public Service Award in 1978 and 1980, and the New Mexico Governor's award for Excellence and Achievement in Literature in 1980. His third novel, *Tortuga*, received the Before Columbus American Book Award in 1980. The script for his play, "Rosa Linda," received a script development award from the Corporation for Public Broadcasting in 1982. In 1983 he received the award for achievement in Chicano literature from the Hispanic Caucus of Teachers of English. In 1986 the Mexican consulate of Albuquerque awarded him the Medal of Friendship. In addition, Anaya has received fellowships from the National Chicano Council on Higher Education, the National Endowment for the Arts, and the Kellogg Foundation.

Bless Me, Ultima (1972) was Anaya's first novel. He based it and subsequent writings on the Spanish-American background of his childhood and youth in New Mexico. Several critics have commented positively on his use of traditional Spanish-American folktales in Bless Me, Ultima. While the novel contains mystical overtones, its main theme is faith and the loss of faith. The protagonist's conflicts come from Anaya's own questioning of beliefs that began while he was a student at the University of New Mexico.

Anaya's second novel, Heart of Aztlán, (1976) is the story of a family's move from rural to urban life. It is more political than his other works, and was not as well-received as *Bless Me, Ultima*.

Tortuga, (1979) his third novel, concerns a young boy who wears a body cast due to paralysis (tortuga is the Spanish word for turtle.) Anaya considers these three novels a trilogy depicting the Hispanic experience in America.

In addition to these novels, Rudolfo Anaya has written plays, screenplays, children's stories and nonfiction essays. He contributes to many periodicals including *La Luz, Bilingual Review-Revista Bilingüe*, and the *Before Columbus Review*. He is the regional editor of *Viaztlán and International Chicano Journal of Arts and Letters*. His manuscript collection is housed at the Zimmerman Museum, University of New Mexico, Albuquerque.

INTRODUCTION

This unit has been designed to develop students' reading, writing, thinking, listening and speaking skills through exercises and activities related to *Bless Me, Ultima* by Rudolfo Anaya. It includes nineteen lessons, supported by extra resource materials.

The **introductory lesson** introduces students to the main themes of the novel: good vs. evil; a struggle with religious beliefs; and choosing a way of life. Following the introductory activity, students are given an explanation of how the activity relates to the book they are about to read.

The **reading assignments** are approximately thirty pages each; some are a little shorter while others are a little longer. Students have approximately 15 minutes of pre-reading work to do prior to each reading assignment. This pre-reading work involves reviewing the study questions for the assignment and doing some vocabulary work for 8 to 10 vocabulary words they will encounter in their reading.

The **study guide questions** are fact-based questions; students can find the answers to these questions right in the text. These questions come in two formats: short answer or multiple choice. The best use of these materials is probably to use the short answer version of the questions as study guides for students (since answers will be more complete), and to use the multiple choice version for occasional quizzes. It might be a good idea to make transparencies of your answer keys for the overhead projector.

The **vocabulary work** is intended to enrich students' vocabularies as well as to aid in the students' understanding of the book. Prior to each reading assignment, students will complete a two-part worksheet for approximately 8 to 10 vocabulary words in the upcoming reading assignment. Part I focuses on students' use of general knowledge and contextual clues by giving the sentence in which the word appears in the text. Students are then to write down what they think the words mean based on the words' usage. Part II gives students dictionary definitions of the words and has them match the words to the correct definitions based on the words' contextual usage. Students should then have an understanding of the words when they meet them in the text. This unit has a supplementary section containing translations of the Spanish phrases used in the novel.

After each reading assignment, students will go back and formulate answers for the study guide questions. Discussion of these questions serves as a **review** of the most important events and ideas presented in the reading assignments.

After students complete extra discussion questions, there is a **vocabulary review** lesson which pulls together all of the separate vocabulary lists for the reading assignments and gives students a review of all of the words they have studied.

Following the reading of the book, two lessons are devoted to the **extra discussion questions/writing assignments**. These questions focus on interpretation, critical analysis and personal response, employing a variety of thinking skills and adding to the students' understanding of the novel. These questions are done as a **group activity**. Using the information they have acquired so far through individual work and class discussions, students get together to further examine the text and to brainstorm ideas relating to the themes of the novel.

The group activity is followed by a **reports and discussion** session in which the groups share their ideas about the book with the entire class; thus, the entire class gets exposed to many different ideas regarding the themes and events of the book.

There are three **writing assignments** in this unit, each with the purpose of informing, persuading, or having students express personal opinions. The first assignment is **inform**. Students will construct a family tree, then write an anecdote about one member of their family. The second assignment is to **persuade**. Students will take the point of view of either the father or the sons, and try to persuade the other to agree with his opinion. The third assignment is to **express personal opinions**. Students will take a stand on whether or not Ultima was a witch.

In addition, there is a **nonfiction reading assignment**. Students are required to read a piece of nonfiction related in some way to *Bless Me, Ultima*. After reading their nonfiction pieces, students will fill out a worksheet on which they answer questions regarding facts, interpretation, criticism, and personal opinions. During one class period, students make **oral presentations** about the nonfiction pieces they have read. This not only exposes all students to a wealth of information, it also gives students the opportunity to practice **public speaking**.

There is an optional **project** (Project Storyteller) through which students will gain knowledge of the folklore of various cultures.

The **review lesson** pulls together all of the aspects of the unit. The teacher is given four or five choices of activities or games to use which all serve the same basic function of reviewing all of the information presented in the unit.

The **unit test** comes in two formats: all multiple choice-matching-true/false or with a mixture of matching, short answer, and composition. As a convenience, two different tests for each format have been included.

There are additional **support materials** included with this unit. The **unit resource section** includes suggestions for an in-class library, crossword and word search puzzles related to the novel, and extra vocabulary worksheets. There is a list of **bulletin board ideas** which gives the teacher suggestions for bulletin boards to go along with this unit. In addition, there is a list of **extra class activities** the teacher could choose from to enhance the unit or as a substitution for an exercise the teacher might feel is inappropriate for his/her class. **Answer keys** are located directly after the **reproducible student materials** throughout the unit. The student materials may be reproduced for use in the teacher's classroom without infringement of copyrights.

UNIT OBJECTIVES *Bless Me, Ultima*

1. Through reading *Bless Me, Ultima,* students will analyze characters and their situations to better understand the themes of the novel.

2. Students will demonstrate their understanding of the text on four levels: factual, interpretive, critical, and personal.

3. Students will practice reading aloud and silently to improve their skills in each area.

4. Students will enrich their vocabularies and improve their understanding of the novel through the vocabulary lessons prepared for use in conjunction with it.

5. Students will answer questions to demonstrate their knowledge and understanding of the main events and characters in *Bless Me, Ultima.*

6. Students will practice writing through a variety of writing assignments.

7. The writing assignments in this are geared to several purposes:
    a. To check the students' reading comprehension
    b. To make students think about the ideas presented by the novel
    c. To make students put those ideas into perspective
    d. To encourage critical and logical thinking
    e. To provide the opportunity to practice good grammar and improve students' use of the English language.

8. Students will read aloud, report, and participate in large and small group discussions to improve their public speaking and personal interaction skills.

UNIT OUTLINE - *Bless Me, Ultima*

1 Unit Intro Distribute Unit Materials PV 1-3 (Uno-Tres)	2 Read 1-3 Study ?? 1-3 Non-Fiction Assignment	3 PVR 4-8 (Cuatro-Ocho) Oral Reading Evaluation	4 Quiz 1-8 PVR 9-10 (Nueve-Diez) Project Introduction	5 Writing Assignment #1
6 Study ?? 9-10 PVR 11-12 (Once-Doce)	7 Study ?? 11-12 PVR 13-14 (Trece-Catorce)	8 Study ?? 13-14 Writing Assignment #2	9 Writing Conference	10 Quiz 9-14 PVR 15-17 (Quince-Diecisiete)
11 Study ?? 15-17 PVR 18-20 (Dieciocho-Veinte)	12 Study ?? 18-20 PVR 21-22 (Veintiuno-Veintidós)	13 Study ?? 21-22	14 Extra Discussion ??	15 Writing Assignment #3
16 Library Work	17 Project Storyteller Presentations	18 Non-Fiction Assignment	19 Vocabulary Review	20 Review
21 Test				

Key: P = Preview Study Questions   V = Vocabulary Work   R = Read

READING ASSIGNMENT SHEET
Bless Me, Ultima

Date to be Assigned	Chapters	Completion Date
	Chapters 1-3 (Uno-Tres)	
	Chapters 4-8 (Cuatro-Ocho)	
	Chapters 9-10 (Nueve-Diez)	
	Chapters 11-12 (Once-Doce)	
	Chapters 13-14 (Trece-Catorce)	
	Chapters 15-17 (Quince-Diecisiete)	
	Chapters 18-20 (Dieciocho-Veinte)	
	Chapters 21-22 (Veintiuno-Veintidós)	

STUDY GUIDE QUESTIONS

SHORT ANSWER STUDY GUIDE QUESTIONS *Bless Me, Ultima*

Chapters 1-3 (Uno-Tres)
1. How old is Antonio when Ultima comes to live with his family?
2. Why does Ultima live with the Márez family?
3. Describe the setting of the novel.
4. Name and describe the members of the Márez family.
5. What was Ultima's occupation?
6. What was the conflict between Gabriel and María concerning Antonio's future?
7. What pet did Ultima bring with her?
8. Describe the incident with Chávez.
9. What did Ultima and the family call Antonio, and why?
10. How did Antonio become a part of the gang with Abel, Bones, and Horse?

Chapters 4-8 (Cuatro-Ocho)
1. How did Ultima feel about plants, the river, and other parts of nature?
2. What did the Márez family always do after supper?
3. How did Ultima describe the Luna and Márez families?
4. Why did Antonio's family go to El Puerto?
5. How did Antonio describe the time spent in El Puerto?
6. How did Antonio feel about going to school?
7. What was Antonio's biggest obstacle in school?
8. What did Antonio discover about his cultural background on the first day of school?
9. What did Gabriel Marez want to do once his sons returned from the war?
10. What did Antonio's brothers talk about doing, and what were their opinions on the subject?

Chapters 9-10 (Nueve-Diez)
1. What was Antonio's dream in Chapter 9 about?
2. What was the conflict between the Márez boys and their parents?
3. In María's opinion, what was the cause of the boys' desires?
4. What did the boys finally do?
5. Antonio asked Andrew if he (Andrew) would become a farmer or a priest. What was Andrew's reply?
6. What happened to Antonio at the end of first grade?
7. Briefly retell Samuel's story of the carp, including the golden carp.
8. What was the supposed cause of Uncle Lucas's illness?
9. Who was Tenorio Trementina?
10. Briefly describe the way Ultima cured Lucas.

Short Answer Study Guide Questions *Bless Me, Ultima*

Chapters 11-12 (Once-Doce)
1. What did Antonio discover about Narciso?
2. How did Antonio feel when he saw the golden carp?
3. What feeling did Antonio and Cico share?
4. How did Cico say the golden carp would punish people?
5. Antonio described his mother's definition of learning to sin. What was it?
6. What did Antonio learn from Ultima's stories?
7. Why were Tenorio and the men coming to the Márez home?
8. What did Narciso say to shame the men who came with Tenorio?
9. Of what did Tenorio accuse Ultima?
10. What was the test for being a witch, and did Ultima pass it?
11. What happened to Tenorio?
12. What did Antonio find on the ground after the men had gone?

Chapters 13-14 (Trece-Catorce)
1. About what was Antonio thinking as the family rode to El Puerto?
2. What happened at the church when Tenorio went to have the mass for the dead and a church burial for his daughter?
3. What was the effect of the priest's stand on Tenorio and the townspeople?
4. What did the Luna uncles request of Antonio's parents?
5. Why did Antonio always look back when he walked away from the house?
6. How did Antonio stop the others from teasing him about Ultima?
7. Briefly describe the Christmas play. What problems arose, and how were they dealt with?
8. Whom did Antonio see as he was walking home from school after the play, and what were they doing?
9. What was Narciso's final destination after the fight, and why?
10. Where did Narciso go on his way to his final destination? Why did he go there, and what was the result of his visit?
11. Describe the fight at the juniper tree. Tell who witnessed it, and what the result of the fight was.
12. What happened after Antonio reached his home?

Short Answer Study Guide Questions *Bless Me, Ultima*

Chapters 15-17 (Quince-Diecisiete)
1. What illness did Antonio get after he saw the murder?
2. What did María tell Antonio would happen when he made his first holy communion?
3. What event broke the monotony of the storm?
4. What was Gabriel's response to his sons' visit, and why?
5. What did Andrew do when León and Eugene left?
6. What did Antonio think about much of the time?
7. What did Antonio think would help him understand his dreams and questions?
8. Whom did Antonio meet on the way home from school, and what happened?
9. The people thought a special event was causing the dust storms and harsh winter. What was the event?
10. What was the topic of the discussion between Florence and Antonio in Chapter 17?

Chapters 18-20 (Dieciocho-Veinte)
1. Who haunted Antonio's nightmares, and why?
2. What did Samuel think would make things easier for Florence?
3. Describe the events that happened when Antonio was on his way to church for his first confession.
4. Florence said he had not sinned, but had been sinned against. Who had sinned against him, and how?
5. What did Antonio expect to happen after he made his first communion, and what really did happen?
6. What did Antonio do every weekend after Easter, and what was the result?
7. Describe the curse on the family near Agua Negra.
8. What was the cause of the curse, according to Ultima?
9. How did Ultima remove the curse?
10. What was Antonio's dream about the night they returned from Agua Negra?

Chapters 21-22 (Veintiuno-Veintidós)
1. What did Cico tell Antonio about God/gods?
2. What did Cico say Antonio's choice was?
3. What happened when the boys went to tell Florence about the golden carp?
4. What did Antonio dream about that night?
5. What did Ultima and Antonio's parents decide he should do for the summer?
6. When Antonio and his father were talking on the way to El Puerto, Gabriel made an unusual statement. What was it?
7. What did Gabriel say understanding was?
8. What trouble occurred in the town later in the summer?
9. What did the uncles plan to do?

Short Answer Study Guide Questions *Bless Me, Ultima*

10. What happened to Antonio on his way back to his Grandfather's house, and what was the result?
11. What did Antonio realize about Ultima's owl?
12. What happened just as Antonio reached his home?
13. What did Ultima ask Antonio to do for her?
14. What did Antonio think abut the upcoming mass of the dead and burial for Ultima?

SHORT ANSWER STUDY GUIDE QUESTIONS WITH ANSWERS *Bless Me, Ultima*

Chapters 1-3 (Uno-Tres)

1. How old is Antonio when Ultima comes to live with his family?
   He is almost seven years old.

2. Why does Ultima live with the Márez family?
   She is getting too old to live alone, and has no one else to take care of her.

3. Describe the setting of the novel.
   The novel is mainly set in the town of Guadalupe, New Mexico. The nearby towns of Las Pasturas and El Puerto de las Lunas are also featured.

4. Name and describe the members of the Márez family.
   Gabriel Márez is the father. He is a vaquero, now living in town and working for the highway department. He still misses his old way of life. María Luna Márez is the mother. She comes from a farming family. Deborah and Teresa are the daughters. They are slightly older than Antonio. León, Andrés, and Eugenio are the older sons who are away fighting in the war. Antonio is the youngest child.

5. What was Ultima's occupation?
   She was a curandera, a woman who uses herbs and ancient ways to cure people.

6. What was the conflict between Gabriel and María concerning Antonio's future?
   Gabriel wanted Antonio to be a vaquero and live on the llano. María wanted him to become a priest, because there had not been a priest in the Luna family for several generations.

7. What pet did Ultima bring with her?
   She brought her pet owl.

8. Describe the incident with Chávez.
   Chávez came to the Márez home, shouting that his brother had been murdered. He asked Gabriel to go with him to search for the murderer, Lupito. Chávez, Gabriel, and other men from the town find Lupito near the river. Narciso tried to reason with him, but the other men shot and killed him.

9. What did Ultima and the family call Antonio, and why?
   He was called the inquisitor, because he asked a lot of questions.

10. How did Antonio become a part of the gang with Abel, Bones, and Horse?
    Horse began to wrestle with Antonio, even though Antonio was much smaller than him. Antonio ducked and then flipped Horse on his back. This gained the respect of Horse and the others, and he was welcomed into the gang.

Chapters 4-8 (Cuatro-Ocho)
1. How did Ultima feel about plants, the river, and other parts of nature?
    She said they all had spirits, and she could feel the presence of the river.

2. What did the Márez family always do after supper?
    They always went into the sala and prayed the rosary in front of the statue of Our Lady of Guadalupe.

3. How did Ultima describe the Luna and Márez families?
    She said the Lunas were quiet like the moon. Their silence enabled them to learn the secrets of the earth that were necessary for planting.

4. Why did Antonio's family go to El Puerto?
    They went to help the Luna family farmers harvest the apple crop.

5. How did Antonio describe the time spent in El Puerto?
    He said they enjoyed the time there. It was a happy place where people worked together and helped each other.

6. How did Antonio feel about going to school?
    He was excited to be learning the magic of the letters, but he was sad to be away from his mother for the first time in his life.

7. What was Antonio's biggest obstacle in school?
    He didn't speak English.

8. What did Antonio discover about his cultural background on the first day of school?
    He discovered that most of the students spoke only English. Since he spoke only Spanish, he could not communicate with them. The other students laughed at his traditional Mexican-style lunch. He felt lonely, and found solace with a few other Mexican-American boys. The group overcame their feelings of loneliness and felt a sense of belonging with each other.

9. What did Gabriel Marez want to do once his sons returned from the war?
    He wanted to move to California.

10. What did Antonio's brothers talk about doing, and what were their opinions on the subject?
    They talked about leaving Guadalupe and going to Las Vegas or another city. Eugene and León were in favor of the move. Andrew was concerned about their father's dream, and wasn't sure he wanted to leave the family.

Chapters 9-10 (Nueve-Diez)
1. What was Antonio's dream in Chapter 9 about?
    He dreamed that he saw his brothers at Rosie's house. He begged them not to enter, but Eugene and León did so anyway. Andrew said he would wait until Antonio lost his innocence. Antonio then wondered about the nature of innocence.

2. What was the conflict between the Márez boys and their parents?
    The boys wanted to move away from home. The parents wanted them to stay in Guadalupe and find work. Gabriel was still holding onto his dream of going to California, but the boys told him they would not go.

3. In María's opinion, what was the cause of the boys' desires?
    She said it was due to the wandering blood of the Márez side of the family.

4. What did the boys finally do?
    Eugene and León left home. Andrew stayed and went back to school.

5. Antonio asked Andrew if he (Andrew) would become a farmer or a priest. What was Andrew's reply?
    Andrew said he and his brothers would not become farmers or priests. He thought maybe the war made them grow up too fast, or they just didn't want to live out their parents' dreams. He told Antonio the he would have to be the one to fit into their parents' dreams.

6. What happened to Antonio at the end of first grade?
    He was promoted to the third grade.

7. Briefly retell Samuel's story of the carp, including the golden carp.
    The townspeople believed it was bad luck to eat the brown carp. According to an old Indian legend, a group known as the people settled in the area, and their gods told them not to eat the carp. After a long drought and famine, they ate the carp, which angered the gods. Most of the gods wanted to kill the people, but one kind god suggested they all be turned into carp. He then asked to be turned into a carp so that he could protect the people. He became the golden carp, the protector of the waters.

8. What was the supposed cause of Uncle Lucas's illness?
    Lucas had seen three witches doing their dance, and had confronted them. They put a curse on him.

9. Who was Tenorio Trementina?
    Tenorio Trementina was the father of the three witches. His wife, now deceased, had been known to work spells. He owned the saloon in El Puerto.

10. Briefly describe the way Ultima cured Lucas.
    She took Antonio with her. First, she went to the saloon to confront Tenorio. She told him to have his daughters lift the curse, but he refused. Then they returned to Lucas's house. They bathed Lucas. Ultima fed him a remedy of kerosene, herbs, and roots. Antonio felt the spasms of his uncle, and shared the struggle against evil with him. Ultima gave Lucas two other liquid remedies. Then she made three clay dolls, dipped them in wax, and dressed them as women. She held the dolls to Lucas's mouth, then stuck a pin in each doll. Ultima then gave Lucas another remedy to drink. After a while, Lucas vomited a hair ball, and then he was cured. Ultima took all of the cloths she had used, and the hairball, and burned them by the tree where the witches did their dance.

Chapters 11-12 (Once-Doce)

1. What did Antonio discover about Narciso?
    Narciso was a very successful gardener. Antonio was amazed at the quality of the fruits and vegetables he produced. He also found out that at planting time Narciso would get drunk and dance as he planted his seeds.

2. How did Antonio feel when he saw the golden carp?
    He trembled, and felt that he had witnessed a miracle. He thought about God's failure and Ultima's success in curing Lucas. The feeling he had when he saw the carp was what he had expected God to do at his first holy communion.

3. What feeling did Antonio and Cico share?
    They felt the presence of the river and the lakes.

4. How did Cico say the golden carp would punish people?
    The town was surrounded by water. The golden carp had warned that the land could not take the weight of the people's sins, and the land would one day sink.

5. Antonio described his mother's definition of learning to sin. What was it?
    She said that losing one's innocence and becoming a man was learning to sin.

6. What did Antonio learn from Ultima's stories?
    He learned the stories and legends of his ancestors. He learned the glory and tragedy of the history of people, and understood how the history stirred in his blood.

7. Why were Tenorio and the men coming to the Márez home?
    Tenorio's daughter died. Tenorio blamed Ultima, and was coming to kill her in revenge.

8. What did Narciso say to shame the men who came with Tenorio?
   He asked them why farmers were out playing vigilantes when they should be home working and relaxing. He also told them they did not need the darkness to hide their deeds. They were ashamed that the town drunk had pointed out their lowly deeds.

9. Of what did Tenorio accuse Ultima?
   He accused her of being a witch, and of killing his daughter.

10. What was the test for being a witch, and did Ultima pass it?
    A witch could not walk through a door marked with the sign of the cross. Ultima walked through the door, and therefore passed the test.

11. What happened to Tenorio?
    Ultima's owl scratched out one of his eyes.

12. What did Antonio find on the ground after the men had gone?
    He found the two needles that had been used to make the cross on the door frame.

Chapters 13-14 (Trece-Catorce)
1. About what was Antonio thinking as the family rode to El Puerto?
   He was wondering why God and the golden carp chose to punish people. He wondered if there could be a forgiving god, and if the Virgin Mary were such a god.

2. What happened at the church when Tenorio went to have the mass for the dead and a church burial for his daughter?
   The priest refused to let him enter the church.

3. What was the effect of the priest's stand on Tenorio and the townspeople?
   Tenorio was not able to influence the people any more. His daughter would have to be buried in unholy ground. Without the mass, her soul would not go to heaven.

4. What did the Luna uncles request of Antonio's parents?
   They wanted Antonio's parents to let him spend the following summer on the farm with them, so they could teach him the ways of the Luna family.

5. Why did Antonio always look back when he walked away from the house?
   He had a feeling that everything would be changed before he got home again.

6. How did Antonio stop the others from teasing him about Ultima?
   He tackled Ernie, the biggest and meanest of the boys. After that they left him alone.

7. Briefly describe the Christmas play. What problems arose, and how were they dealt with?
   There was so much snow that many of the children stayed home from school. The boys who were there had to take all of the parts, including the girls' parts. Bones climbed a stage rope, sat on a beam, and refused to come down. Miss Violet offered to give Horse an A if he would play the Virgin Mary. Abel had to use the bathroom, but Miss Violet would not let him. After the play started, he wet his pants. The Kid slipped in Abel's urine, and the audience got hysterical. The scenery started falling over. Bones came down from the rafters and landed on Horse. Florence hit the light bulb and broke it.

8. Whom did Antonio see as he was walking home from school after the play, and what were they doing?
   He saw Tenorio and Narciso fighting as they came out of the bar. The bartender and a few other men pulled them apart, and each left the area.

9. What was Narciso's final destination after the fight, and why?
   He was going to the Márez home to warn Ultima that Tenorio was again going to try and kill her. Tenorio's second daughter was dying, and Tenorio blamed it on Ultima.

10. Where did Narciso go on his way to his final destination? Why did he go there, and what was the result of his visit?
    He went to Rosies to get help from Andrew. Andrew didn't take Narciso seriously, and refused to go with him.

11. Describe the fight at the juniper tree. Tell who witnessed it, and what the result of the fight was.
    Antonio witnessed the whole event. Tenorio shot Narciso. Tenorio saw Antonio, but left him alone. Antonio heard Narciso's confession, and Narciso died. Then Antonio ran home to get help.

12. What happened after Antonio reached his home?
    He got a fever and had nightmares. Gabriel went to tend to Narciso.

<u>Chapters 15-17 (Quince-Diecisiete)</u>

1. What illness did Antonio get after he saw the murder?
   He got pneumonia.

2. What did María tell Antonio would happen when he made his first holy communion?
   She said he would hold God in his mouth, his body, and his soul. Antonio would speak to God, and God would answer.

3. What event broke the monotony of the storm?
　　León and Eugene arrived.

4. What was Gabriel's response to his sons' visit, and why?
　　He got drunk. He had heard them planning to leave, and he knew they would not go to California with him.

5. What did Andrew do when León and Eugene left?
　　He went with them this time.

6. What did Antonio think about much of the time?
　　He thought about the dreams he had during his illness. He wondered why Narciso, who was good, was killed and Tenorio went unpunished. He asked God to answer his questions.

7. What did Antonio think would help him understand his dreams and questions?
　　He thought he would understand after he made his communion.

8. Whom did Antonio meet on the way home from school, and what happened?
　　He met Tenorio. Tenorio told him his second daughter was dying, and he would find a way to kill Ultima.

9. The people thought a special event was causing the dust storms and harsh winter. What was the event?
　　They blamed the dust storms and harsh winter on the atomic bomb that had been exploded to the south of them.

10. What was the topic of the discussion between Florence and Antonio in Chapter 17?
　　They were discussing sin and forgiveness, why bad things happen to good people, and why Florence was going to catechism when he was not a Catholic.

Chapters 18-20 (Dieciocho-Veinte)
1. Who haunted Antonio's nightmares, and why?
　　Antonio dreamed about Florence. He dreamed that Florence was damned forever because he did not accept God.

2. What did Samuel think would make things easier for Florence?
　　He thought it would be easier if Florence believed in the golden carp.

3. Describe the events that happened when Antonio was on his way to church for his first confession.
   The other boys forced him to hear their confessions. When Florence refused to go to confession and said he didn't have any sins, the other boys got angry. Antonio defended Florence, and the boys turned on him. Horse jumped on his chest while the others held Antonio down and hit him.

4. Florence said he had not sinned, but had been sinned against. Who had sinned against him, and how?
   Florence said God had sinned against him, because God had taken away both of his parents and made his sisters whores. He said God had punished all of them without cause.

5. What did Antonio expect to happen after he made his first communion, and what really did happen?
   He expected to hear God telling him the answers to all of his questions. In reality, the host was sticky, and the only things he felt were hunger and emptiness.

6. What did Antonio do every weekend after Easter, and what was the result?
   He went to confession on Saturday and communion on Sunday. He was still dissatisfied, because the God he looked for was not there.

7. Describe the curse on the family near Agua Negra.
   The Téllez family had dishes and utensils crashing and falling. There were stones falling from the sky and pelting the house.

8. What was the cause of the curse, according to Ultima?
   The grandfather of Téllez had hanged three Comanche Indians on the property, but did not give them a proper burial. Ultima said it was their spirits haunting the place.

9. How did Ultima remove the curse?
   She had Gabriel and Téllez build a Comanche funeral platform. She placed three bundles on it and had the men set it all on fire. When all had burned, she said the curse was lifted.

10. What was Antonio's dream about the night they returned from Agua Negra?
    He dreamed about his three brothers. They were asking him to help them rest from their sea-blood. He took their livers and threw them into the River of the Carp. His brothers rested after that.

Chapters 21-22 (Veintiuno-Veintidós)
1. What did Cico tell Antonio about God/gods?
   He said there were many gods-of beauty, of magic, of garden and backyards. People searched in the stars and foreign countries to find new ones.

2. What did Cico say Antonio's choice was?
   Antonio had to choose between the God of the church and the beauty of the here and now.

3. What happened when the boys went to tell Florence about the golden carp?
   They found out that he had dived into the water and had not come up. Cico and Antonio went in after him. By the time they pulled him out he was already dead.

4. What did Antonio dream about that night?
   He dreamed about Narciso, Lupito, and Florence. He saw a priest desecrating an altar with pigeons' blood, Cico killing the golden carp, and Tenorio killing Ultima's night-spirit.

5. What did Ultima and Antonio's parents decide he should do for the summer?
   They agreed that he should spend the summer with the Lunas on their farm.

6. When Antonio and his father were talking on the way to El Puerto, Gabriel made an unusual statement. What was it?
   He commented that it might be time to give up the old differences between the Márez and Luna ways.

7. What did Gabriel say understanding was?
   He said it was having sympathy for people.

8. What trouble occurred in the town later in the summer?
   Tenorio's daughter died. Tenorio stretched her body out on the bar of his saloon. Then he got drunk and yelled about getting revenge on Ultima.

9. What did the uncles plan to do?
   Pedro said he would take Antonio and drive to Guadalupe to warn Ultima as soon as they were finished in the fields.

10. What happened to Antonio on his way back to his Grandfather's house, and what was the result?
    He met Tenorio, who was drunk and on horseback. Tenorio tried to run him down. Antonio evaded him, got scared, and started running back to Guadalupe to warn Ultima.

11. What did Antonio realize about Ultima's owl?
    He realized that it was her spirit.

12. What happened just as Antonio reached his home?
    He saw Tenorio hiding near the juniper tree. Tenorio shot and killed the owl. Then Pedro shot Tenorio and killed him.

13. What did Ultima ask Antonio to do for her?
    She asked him to bury the owl's body and bury it under a certain forked juniper tree. She also asked him to clean out her room the following day and burn all of her medicine and herbs near the river.

14. What did Antonio think abut the upcoming mass of the dead and burial for Ultima?
    He thought they were just the ceremony that was required by custom. She was really buried under the juniper tree.

MULTIPLE CHOICE STUDY GUIDE/QUIZ QUESTIONS *Bless Me, Ultima*

Chapters 1-3 (Uno-Tres)

1. How old is Antonio when Ultima comes to live with his family?
    A. He is fifteen years old.
    B. He is a baby, only a few months old.
    C. He is almost seven years old.
    D. He is ten years old.

2. Why does Ultima live with the Márez family?
    A. She comes to help María, who is no longer able to care for the family.
    B. Her house in Las Pasturas burned down and she doesn't have anywhere to live.
    C. She is Antonio's godmother, and wants to make sure he is taken care of.
    D. She is getting too old to live alone, and has no one else to take care of her.

3. Which of the following towns is **not** mentioned in the novel?
    A. Guadalupe
    B. Las Pasturas
    C. El Puerto de la Luna
    D. Gonzales

4. What are the names of Antonio's brothers and sisters?
    A. León, Andrés, Eugenio, Deborah, and Theresa
    B. León, Andrés, Eduardo, Deborah, and Theresa
    C. Lorenzo, Andrés, Eduardo, Deborah, and Theresa
    D. Lorenzo, Angel, Eduardo, Dolores, and Theresa

5. True or False: Ultima was one of the only Mexican-American doctors in the area.
    A. True
    B. False

6. True or False: María wanted Antonio to become a farmer and live in Las Pasturas.
    A. True
    B. False

7. What pet did Ultima bring with her?
    A. She brought her black cat.
    B. She brought a pet coyote.
    C. She brought a trained bat.
    D. She brought her pet owl.

Multiple Choice Questions *Bless Me, Ultima*

8. Which of the following did **not** happen when Chávez came to the Márez home?
    A. Chávez shouted that his brother had been murdered.
    B. They found Lupito near the juniper tree.
    C. Chávez, Gabriel, and other men from the town went on the search.
    D. Narciso tried to reason with Lupito, but the other men shot and killed him.

9. What did Ultima and the family call Antonio, and why?
    A. They called him the inquisitor, because he asked a lot of questions.
    B. They called him the holy one, because they wanted him to be a priest.
    C. They called him the professor, because he was so smart.
    D. They called him the baby, because he was the youngest in the family.

10. Whom did Antonio wrestle and flip to become a part of the gang?
    A. It was Bones.
    B. It was Abel.
    C. It was the Vitamin Kid.
    D. It was Horse.

Multiple Choice Study Guide/Quiz Questions *Bless Me, Ultima*

Chapters 4-8 (Cuatro-Ocho)

1. What was Ultima talking about when she said she could feel its presence?
    A. the river
    B. the owl
    C. evil
    D. the moon

2. What did the Márez family always do after supper?
    A. They listened to Gabriel tell stories of the old days.
    B. They went for a long walk.
    C. They went into the sala and prayed the rosary in front of the statue of Our Lady of Guadalupe.
    D. The children did their homework, María did the dishes, and Gabriel got drunk.

3. True or False: Ultima said the Márez clan members were quiet like the moon. Their silence enabled them to learn the secrets of the earth that were necessary for planting.
    A. True
    B. False

4. Why did Antonio's family go to El Puerto?
    A. They went to help the Luna family farmers harvest the apple crop.
    B. They went to help round up the calves and brand them.
    C. They went to celebrate María's father's birthday.
    D. They went to attend the Mass celebrating the founding of the town.

5. How did Antonio describe the time spent in El Puerto?
    A. He said it was hard work that he didn't like.
    B. He said he realized that he did not want to be a farmer.
    C. He said it was unpleasant because everyone fought.
    D. He said it was a happy place where people worked together.

6. How did Antonio feel about going to school?
    A. He was scared and didn't want to go.
    B. He was glad to be getting away from the house.
    C. He was excited to be learning the magic of the letters, but he was sad to be away from his mother for the first time in his life.
    D. He wanted to learn, but was afraid he would fail and disappoint his parents.

Multiple Choice Questions *Bless Me, Ultima*

7. What was Antonio's biggest obstacle in school?
    A. He was younger than all of the other children.
    B. He needed glasses, and couldn't see the board.
    C. He had a long walk. By the time he got to school, he was too tired to learn.
    D. He didn't speak English.

8. True or False: On Antonio's first day of school he felt lonely, and found solace with a few other Mexican-American boys.
    A. True
    B. False

9. What did Gabriel Marez want to do once his sons returned from the war?
    A. He wanted to buy more land and start a farm.
    B. He wanted to move to California.
    C. He wanted to go back to the llano and raise cattle.
    D. He wanted to retire and let his sons support him.

10. Antonio's brothers talked about leaving Guadalupe and going to Las Vegas or another city. What were their opinions?
    A. Eugene and Andrew wanted to move. León didn't want to leave the family.
    B. They all wanted to move.
    C. Eugene and León were in favor of the move. Andrew was concerned about their father's dream, and wasn't sure he wanted to leave the family.
    D. Only Eugene wanted to move.

Multiple Choice Study Guide/Quiz Questions *Bless Me, Ultima*

Chapters 9-10 (Nueve-Diez)
1. Where were Antonio's brothers in the dream in Chapter 9?
    A. They were in California.
    B. They were in heaven.
    C. They were overseas in the war.
    D. They were at Rosie's house.

2. True or False: Gabriel and María supported their sons' desires to move away.
    A. True
    B. False

3. In María's opinion, what was the cause of the boys' desires?
    A. She said the war ruined them.
    B. She said it was due to the wandering blood of the Márez side of the family.
    C. She said it was because they never went to church.
    D. She said their father's drinking was driving them away from home.

4. What did the boys finally do?
    A. Eugene and León left home. Andrew stayed and went back to school.
    B. Eugene and Andrew left home. León went to work on the highway.
    C. Andrew and León left home. Eugene stayed home, but did not work.
    D. They all left home.

5. True or False: When Antonio asked Andrew if he (Andrew) would become a farmer or a priest, Andrew said he would probably end up a vaquero like his father.
    A. True
    B. False

6. What happened to Antonio at the end of first grade?
    A. He failed and was told he would have to repeat the next year.
    B. He got the medal for the most improved.
    C. He liked his teacher so much he refused to go to second grade.
    D. He was promoted to the third grade.

Multiple Choice Questions *Bless Me, Ultima*

7. Which of the following statements was **not** included in Samuel's story of the carp?
   A. According to an old Indian legend, a group known as the people settled in the area, and their gods told them not to eat the carp.
   B. After a long drought and famine, they ate the carp, which angered the gods.
   C. Most of the gods wanted to turn the people into carp.
   D. One god turned into the golden carp, the protector of the waters.

8. What was the supposed cause of Uncle Lucas's illness?
   A. Lucas had seen three witches doing their dance, and had confronted them. They put a curse on him.
   B. He had committed a mortal sin and refused to go to confession.
   C. He had cancer but the doctors there didn't understand how to treat it.
   D. He had walked through an Indian burial ground and was being haunted by the spirits who lived there.

9. Which of the following does **not** describe Tenorio?
   A. Tenorio was the father of the three witches.
   B. His wife, now deceased, had been known to work spells.
   C. He owned the saloon in El Puerto.
   D. He was very rich and well-respected in the town.

10. Which of the following was **not** used in Ultima's cure of Lucas?
    A. She bathed Lucas.
    B. Ultima fed him a remedy of turpentine, herbs, and roots.
    C. She made three clay dolls, dipped them in wax, and dressed them as women. She held the dolls to Lucas's mouth, then stuck a pin in each doll.
    D. After a while, Lucas vomited a hairball, and then he was cured.

Multiple Choice Quiz/Study Guide Questions *Bless Me, Ultima*

Chapters 11-12 (Once-Doce)
1. What did Antonio discover about Narciso?
   A. He was an artist who painted lovely scenes of the area.
   B. He was a gifted musician.
   C. Narciso was a very successful gardener.
   D. He loved cats. He had twelve of them in his house.

2. True or False: The feeling Antonio had when he saw the carp was what he had expected God to do at his first holy communion.
   A. True
   B. False

3. With whom did Antonio share his feelings about the presence of the river?
   A. Bones
   B. Cico
   C. Florence
   D. Andrew

4. True or False: Cico said The town was built on an earthquake fault line. The golden carp had warned that the land could not take the weight of the people's sins, and the weight would one day cause an earthquake that would swallow the town.
   A. True
   B. False

5. Antonio described his mother's definition of learning to sin. What was it?
   A. She said it was having bad thoughts.
   B. She said it was refusing to go to confession and communion.
   C. She said that losing one's innocence and becoming a man was learning to sin.
   D. She said it was doing what others said without thinking.

6. What did Antonio learn from Ultima's stories?
   A. He learned the stories and legends of his ancestors.
   B. He learned how to be a curandero.
   C. He learned about Ultima's childhood.
   D. He learned the history of the area.

Multiple Choice Questions *Bless Me, Ultima*

7. Why were Tenorio and the men coming to the Márez home?
    A. Tenorio wanted Ultima to cure his daughter, who was ill.
    B. Tenorio said the priest had sent him to get rid of Ultima.
    C. Tenorio's daughter wanted to become a curandera.
    D. Tenorio's daughter died. Tenorio blamed Ultima, and was coming to kill her in revenge.

8. Who shamed the men who came with Tenorio?
    A. Ultima
    B. Narciso
    C. Antonio
    D. Gabriel

9. Of what did Tenorio accuse Ultima?
    A. He said she was a devil.
    B. He said she was a heathen.
    C. He said she was a ghoul.
    D. He accused her of being a witch.

10. What was the test that Tenorio made Ultima take?
    A. She had to say the rosary out loud.
    B. She had to bless herself with holy water.
    C. She had to walk through a door marked with the sign of the cross.
    D. She had to go to take holy communion.

11. What happened to Tenorio?
    A. He fainted from exhaustion.
    B. He failed the test he was giving Ultima.
    C. He got sick while Ultima was taking the test.
    D. Ultima's owl scratched out one of his eyes.

12. True or False: After the men had gone, Antonio found three owl's feathers in a triangular shape to the left of the door frame.
    A. True
    B. False

Multiple Choice Study Guide/Quiz Questions *Bless Me, Ultima*

Chapters 13-14 (Trece-Catorce)

1. Antonio was thinking as the family rode to El Puerto. Which of the following was **not** in his thoughts?
    A. He wondered which was more powerful-his God or the golden carp.
    B. He was wondering why God and the golden carp chose to punish people.
    C. He wondered if there could be a forgiving God.
    D. He wondered if the Virgin Mary was forgiving or punitive.

2. True or False: The priest agreed to let Tenorio have the mass for the dead and a church burial for his daughter?
    A. True
    B. False

3. What was the effect of the priest's stand on Tenorio and the townspeople?
    A. The people lost faith in the priest and asked him to leave town.
    B. Tenorio had more influence on the people.
    C. Tenorio was not able to influence the people any more.
    D. The townspeople hated both the priest and Tenorio.

4. True or False: The Luna uncles wanted Antonio's parents to let him spend the following summer on the farm with them, so they could teach him the ways of the Luna family.
    A. True
    B. False

5. Why did Antonio always look back when he walked away from the house?
    A. He thought it would bring him good luck.
    B. He wanted to see if his mother was waving to him.
    C. He looked to see if Ultima's owl was nearby to protect her.
    D. He had a feeling that everything would be changed before he got home again.

6. How did Antonio stop the others from teasing him about Ultima?
    A. He tackled Ernie, the biggest and meanest of the boys.
    B. He threatened to have Ultima put a curse on them.
    C. He said he would tell the priest they were sinning.
    D. He brought his father's gun one day and said he would shoot them.

Multiple Choice Questions *Bless Me, Ultima*

7. Which of the following did **not** happen during the Christmas play?
    A. Horse played the Virgin Mary.
    B. Bones threw things at the audience.
    C. Abel wet his pants.
    D. Florence hit the light bulb and broke it.

8. Whom did Antonio see as he was walking home from school after the play?
    A. He saw Narciso going into the bar carrying a shotgun.
    B. He saw Tenorio riding down the street on his horse, swinging a whip.
    C. He saw Tenorio and Narciso fighting as they came out of the bar.
    D. He saw Narciso and a group of men chasing Tenorio out of town.

9. What was Narciso's final destination after the incident in the bar with Tenorio and why?
    A. He was going to the sheriff's office to get a warrant for Tenorio's arrest.
    B. He was going home to tend to his wounds.
    C. He was going to the church to ask for help from the priest.
    D. He was going to the Márez home to warn Ultima that Tenorio was on his way.

10. True or False: Andrew left Rosie's and went with Narciso.
    A. True
    B. False

11. What happened at the juniper tree?
    A. Narciso killed Tenorio.
    B. Tenorio put a curse on Narciso, then went home.
    C. Tenorio killed Narciso.
    D. The sheriff got there in time and stopped the fight.

12. What happened after Antonio reached his home?
    A. He got a fever and had nightmares.
    B. Ultima went out to talk to Tenorio and Narciso.
    C. He was so frightened he couldn't talk for a week.
    D. María made him say the rosary three times.

Multiple Choice Study Guide/Quiz Questions   *Bless Me, Ultima*

Chapters 15-17 (Quince-Diecisiete)
1. What illness did Antonio get after he saw the murder?
    A. He got amnesia.
    B. He got bronchitis.
    C. He got pneumonia.
    D. He became severely depressed.

2. True or False: María said that when Antonio made his first communion, he would speak to God, and God would answer.
    A. True
    B. False

3. What event broke the monotony of the storm?
    A. The Luna uncles came for a visit.
    B. Ultima told stories about the past.
    C. María, Ultima, and Antonio baked cookies.
    D. León and Eugene arrived.

4. What was Gabriel's response to his sons' visit?
    A. He refused to let them in the house.
    B. He got drunk.
    C. He welcomed them joyfully, and said they should do what they wanted.
    D. He held a party in their honor.

5. What did Andrew do when León and Eugene left?
    A. He got a job with the highway.
    B. He went with them this time.
    C. He told his father he would go to California.
    D. He got drunk and went to Rosie's.

6. What did Antonio think about much of the time?
    A. He wondered what he would be when he grew up.
    B. He worried about Ultima.
    C. He thought about the dreams he had during his illness.
    D. He wondered why his parents ever got married, when they were so different.

Multiple Choice Questions *Bless Me, Ultima*

7. What did Antonio think would help him understand his dreams and questions?
    A. He thought he would understand after he made his communion.
    B. He thought he would understand if Ultima taught him.
    C. He thought he would understand when he was as old as his brothers.
    D. He thought losing his innocence would help him understand.

8. Whom did Antonio meet on the way home from school, and what happened?
    A. He met Cico and they went to see the golden carp.
    B. He met Andrew, and they went to Rosie's together.
    C. He met his father and they had a good talk on the way home.
    D. He met Tenorio. Tenorio told him his second daughter was dying, and he would find a way to kill Ultima.

9. The people thought a special event was causing the dust storms and harsh winter. What was the event?
    A. They blamed it on the atomic bomb that had been exploded to the south of them.
    B. They said Tenorio was casting a spell on them.
    C. They thought Ultima was doing it to rid the area of demons.
    D. They thought God was displeased with the fighting in their communities.

10. What was the topic of the discussion between Florence and Antonio in Chapter 17?
    A. They were discussing what they would do over the summer.
    B. They were discussing what they thought the host would taste like.
    C. They were discussing who would probably fail the catechism lessons.
    D. They were discussing sin and forgiveness.

Multiple Choice Study Guide/Quiz Questions   *Bless Me, Ultima*

<u>Chapters 18-20 (Dieciocho-Veinte)</u>

1. Who haunted Antonio's nightmares?
    A. He dreamed about Florence.
    B. He dreamed about Samuel.
    C. He dreamed about Ultima.
    D. He dreamed about his brothers.

2. What did Samuel think would make things easier for Florence?
    A. He thought it would be easier if his parents would adopt Florence.
    B. He thought it would be easier if Florence would become Catholic.
    C. He thought it would be easier if Florence believed in the golden carp.
    D. He thought it would be easier if Florence moved to another town.

3. Which of the following describes one of the events that happened when Antonio was on his way to church for his first confession?
    A. He thought he saw a vision of the Virgin Mary.
    B. The other boys forced him to hear their confessions.
    C. Horse beat up Bones.
    D. Florence said he was going to make his communion along with the others.

4. One of the boys said he had not sinned, but had been sinned against. He said God had sinned against him, because god had taken away both of his parents and made his sisters whores. He said God had punished all of them without cause. Which boy was it?
    A. It was Bones.
    B. It was Abel.
    C. It was Cico.
    D. It was Florence.

5. Antonio expected to hear God telling him the answers to all of his questions after he made his first communion. Did this really happen?
    A. Yes, it did.
    B. No, it didn't.

6. What did Antonio do every weekend after Easter?
    A. He went to confession on Saturday and communion on Sunday.
    B. He went to see the golden carp.
    C. He went to Narciso's grave and prayed for him.
    D. He studied plants and herbs with Ultima.

Multiple Choice Questions *Bless Me, Ultima*

7. Describe the curse on the Téllez family near Agua Negra.
    A. Any food they kept in the house went bad almost immediately.
    B. They were all covered with boils, blisters, and rashes that would not heal.
    C. Dishes and utensils were crashing and falling. Stones were falling from the sky.
    D. They could hear someone wailing and crying, but could not see anyone.

8. True or False: According to Ultima, the grandfather of Téllez had hanged three Comanche Indians on the property, but did not give them a proper burial. Ultima said it was their spirits haunting the place.
    A. True
    B. False

9. How did Ultima remove the curse?
    A. She went to the Comanche reservation and asked the chief for forgiveness.
    B. She built a ring of yerba buena around the house to keep the spirits away.
    C. She made three dolls and buried them in the ground near the house.
    D. She had Gabriel and Téllez build a Comanche funeral platform. She placed three bundles on it and had the men set it all on fire. When all had burned, she said the
    curse was lifted.

10. Antonio's dream the night they returned from Agua Negra was about his brothers. What did he do to help them?
    A. He went to Rosie's and made all of the girls go to confession and communion.
    B. He took their livers and threw them into the River of the Carp. His brothers rested after that.
    C. He told them not to worry, that he would take care of their parents.
    D. He used some of Ultima's powers to take away the painful war memories.

Multiple Choice Study Guide/Quiz Questions *Bless Me, Ultima*

Chapters 21-22 (Veintiuno-Veintidós)

1. What did Cico tell Antonio about God/gods?
    A. He said there was no god at all, only beings imagined by people.
    B. He said the golden carp was the only true god.
    C. He said there were many gods-of beauty, of magic, of garden and backyards.
    D. He said there was only on God, but he had many forms.

2. True or False: Cico said Antonio had to choose between the god of the church and the beauty of the here and now.
    A. True
    B. False

3. What happened when the boys went to tell Florence about the golden carp?
    A. He was glad to hear it, and went with them to see the carp.
    B. He invited them to swim with him.
    C. He said he already knew all about it.
    D. They found out that he had dived into the water and had not come up.

4. Which of the following was not in Antonio's dream that night?
    A. He dreamed about Narciso, Lupito, and Florence.
    B. He saw Cico turning into the golden carp.
    C. He saw a priest desecrating an altar with pigeons' blood.
    D. He saw Tenorio killing Ultima's night-spirit.

5. What did Ultima and Antonio's parents decide he should do for the summer?
    A. They were going to send him to stay with his brothers.
    B. They thought he should study with Ultima every day.
    C. They agreed that he should spend the summer with the Lunas on their farm.
    D. They decided to send him to a seminary in Las Cruces.

6. True or False: When Antonio and his father were talking on the way to El Puerto, Gabriel commented that it might be time to give up the old differences between the Márez and Luna ways.
    A. True
    B. False

Multiple Choice Questions *Bless Me, Ultima*

7. What did Gabriel say understanding was?
    A. He said it was losing the innocence of childhood.
    B. He said it was knowing and doing the right thing.
    C. He said it was loving someone no matter what they did.
    D. He said it was having sympathy for people.

8. What trouble occurred in the town later in the summer?
    A. The priest tried to make Ultima move out of town.
    B. Tenorio's daughter died.
    C. Narciso's brother came to get revenge on Tenorio.
    D. The boys formed a gang and started terrorizing the townspeople.

9. What did the uncles plan to do?
    A. They told Antonio to walk back to his home.
    B. They said they would not do anything.
    C. Pedro said he would take Antonio and drive to Guadalupe.
    D. They went after Tenorio.

10. What happened to Antonio on his way back to his Grandfather's house?
    A. Tenorio tried to run him down.
    B. He saw Narciso's ghost.
    C. The owl tried to scare Tenorio's horse.
    D. His uncle picked him up and gave him a ride.

11. What did Antonio realize about Ultima's spirit?
    A. He realized it was the same as the presence of the river.
    B. He realized she had put it in him.
    C. He realized that it was powerful and would live forever.
    D. He realized that it was the owl.

12. What happened just as Antonio reached his home?
    A. Gabriel killed Tenorio.
    B. Tenorio shot and killed the owl.
    C. Ultima put a curse on Tenorio and he died.
    D. Tenorio shot Ultima.

Multiple Choice Questions *Bless Me, Ultima*

13. True or False: Ultima gave all of her herbs and potions to Antonio. She made him promise to continue her work and become a curandero.
    A. True
    B. False

14. What did Antonio think about the upcoming mass of the dead and burial for Ultima?
    A. He thought they proved beyond a doubt that she was not a witch.
    B. They gave him a sense of finality about her death.
    C. He thought they were just the ceremony that was required by custom.
    D. He thought it was wrong to do them, because she never said she wanted them.

ANSWER KEY: MULTIPLE CHOICE STUDY GUIDE/QUIZ QUESTIONS *Bless Me, Ultima*

Chapters 1-3
1. C
2. D
3. B
4. A
5. B False
6. C
7. D
8. B
9. A
10. D

Chapters 4-8
1. A
2. C
3. B False
4. A
5. D
6. C
7. D
8. A True
9. B
10. C

Chapters 9-10
1. D
2. B False
3. B
4. A
5. B False
6. D
7. C
8. A
9. D
10. B

Chapters 11-12
1. C
2. A True
3. D
4. B False
5. C
6. B False
7. D
8. B
9. D
10. C
11. D
12. B False

Chapters 13-14
1. A
2. B False
3. C
4. A True
5. D
6. A
7. B
8. C
9. D
10. B False
11. C
12. A

Chapters 15-17
1. C
2. A True
3. D
4. B
5. B
6. C
7. A
8. D
9. A
10. D

Chapters 18-20
1. A
2. C
3. B
4. D
5. B No
6. A
7. C
8. A True
9. D
10. B

Chapters 21-22
1. C   11. D
2. A   12. B
3. D   13. B False
4. B   14. C
5. C
6. A True
7. D
8. B
9. C
10. A

PREREADING VOCABULARY WORKSHEETS

Vocabulary Worksheets *Bless Me, Ultima*

Chapters 1-3
Part I: Using Prior Knowledge and Context Clues
Below are the sentences in which the vocabulary words appear in the text. Read the sentence. Use any clues you can find in the sentence combined with your prior knowledge, and write what you think the underlined words mean on the lines provided.

1. The move lowered my father in the esteem of his compadres, the other vaqueros of the llano who clung *tenaciously* to their way of life and freedom.

   _____

2. They were an *exuberant*, restless people, wandering across the ocean of the plain.

   _____

3. During the day she would *forage* along the highway where the grass was thick and green, then she would return at nightfall.

   _____

4. Always on the move, like gypsies, always dragging their families around the country like *vagabonds*.

   _____

5. My nostrils quivered as I felt the song of the mockingbirds and the *drone* of the grasshoppers mingle with the pulse of the earth.

   _____

6. . . . they had more time to spend in the attic and cut out and *interminable* train of paper dolls which they dressed, gave names to, and, most miraculously, made talk.

   _____

7. My father shook Chávez and the man's sobbing *subsided*.

   _____

Vocabulary Worksheets *Bless Me, Ultima*

8. They stood *transfixed*, looking down at the mad man waving the pistol in the air.
   _____

9. The cry of a *tormented* man had come to the peaceful green mystery of my river . . . .
   _____

10. Again the owl sang; Ultima's spirit bathed me with its strong *resolution*.
    _____

11. I lay back and watched the silent beams of light radiate in the colorful dust *motes* I had stirred up.
    _____

12. Also, my mother *admonished* us to bow our heads when we passed in front of the house.
    _____

Part II: Determining the Meaning Match the vocabulary words to their dictionary definitions.

_____ 1. tenaciously   A. became less agitated or active
_____ 2. exuberant   B. joyous; full of high spirits
_____ 3. forage   C. rendered motionless
_____ 4. vagabonds   D. people without permanent homes
_____ 5. drone   E. firm determination
_____ 6. interminable   F. endless
_____ 7. subsided   G. holding persistently to something
_____ 8. transfixed   H. caused to undergo great pain or anguish
_____ 9. tormented   I. a continuous low dull humming sound
_____ 10. resolutions   J. to wander in search of food or provisions
_____ 11. motes   K. very small particles; specks
_____ 12. admonished   L. reproved gently but earnestly

Vocabulary Worksheets *Bless Me, Ultima*

Chapters 4-8
Part I: Using Prior Knowledge and Context Clues
Below are the sentences in which the vocabulary words appear in the text. Read the sentence. Use any clues you can find in the sentence combined with your prior knowledge, and write what you think the underlined words mean on the lines provided.

1. Of all the plants we gathered none was **endowed** with so much magic as the yerba del manso.

   _____

2. I ran to the cactus and gathered a shovelful of the *succulent*, seedy pears.

   _____

3. We all knew the story of how the Virgin had presented herself to the little Indian boy in Mexico and about the miracles she had *wrought*.

   _____

4. Her soul was without *blemish*.

   _____

5. "¡Vamos! ¡Vamos!" my uncle called and we *clamored* aboard.

   _____

6. She was soon lost in the *furrow* of dust the truck raised.

   _____

7. I had never felt such fear before, because as the whirlwind blew its *debris* around be the gushing wind seemed to call my name: Antonioooooooooooooooo . . . .

   _____

Vocabulary Worksheets *Bless Me, Ultima*

8. I was held hypnotized by the thundering herd, then with a cry of resolution exploding from my throat I rushed into the *melee*.

   _____

9. His forwardness and *audacity* often caught them off guard.

   _____

10. His voiced *quavered*. His excitement carried to his brothers.

    _____

Part II: Determining the Meaning   Match the vocabulary words to their dictionary definitions.

_____ 1. endowed   A. made a loud, sustained noise or outcry
_____ 2. succulent   B. put together; created
_____ 3. wrought   C. rubble or wreckage
_____ 4. blemish   D. trembled
_____ 5. clamored   E. fearlessness; boldness
_____ 6. furrow   F. a rut, groove, or narrow depression
_____ 7. debris   G. an imperfection that mars or impairs
_____ 8. melee   H. full of juice or sap; juicy.
_____ 9. audacity   I. provided with property or income
_____ 10. quavered   J. a violent free-for-all

Vocabulary Worksheets *Bless Me, Ultima*

Chapters 9-10
Part I: Using Prior Knowledge and Context Clues
Below are the sentences in which the vocabulary words appear in the text. Read the sentence. Use any clues you can find in the sentence combined with your prior knowledge, and write what you think the underlined words mean on the lines provided.

1. I opened my eyes and heard the *commotion* downstairs.
   _____

2. They knew that it was within the power of the father to curse his sons, and ay! a curse laid on a disobedient son or daughter was *irrevocable*.
   _____

3. "You are *forsaking* me," my mother cried afresh.
   _____

4. "Ay, Márez men," she said *stoically* and turned to my father.
   _____

5. Even the holy priest at El Puerto had been asked to *exorcise* el encanto, the curse, and he had failed.
   _____

6. The rancher swore that he had *etched* a cross on his bullet, and that proved that the old woman was a witch, and so he was let free.
   _____

7. Then they began to cook it, throwing in many other things while they danced and chanted their *incantations*.
   _____

Vocabulary Worksheets *Bless Me, Ultima*

8. "No, I will be proud, Ultima," I said *emphatically*.

   _____

9. The eyes were dark and narrow. An evil glint *emanated from* them.

   _____

10. Instead of sleep I slipped into a deep *stupor*.

    _____

11. I suffered the spasms of pain my uncle suffered, and these alternated with feelings of *elation* and power.

    _____

12. The *acrid* smell of the dark yellow pee blended into the fragrance of the cereal.

    _____

Part II: Determining the Meaning   Match the vocabulary words to their dictionary definitions.

____ 1.	commotion	A.	cut into the surface of
____ 2.	irrevocable	B.	giving up something formerly held dear
____ 3.	forsaking	C.	mental numbness from shock; a daze
____ 4.	stoically	D.	positively; definitely
____ 5.	exorcise	E.	impossible to retract or withdraw
____ 6.	etched	F.	unpleasantly sharp, pungent, or bitter to smell
____ 7.	incantation	G.	came or sent forth, as from a source
____ 8.	emphatically	H.	pride; joy
____ 9.	emanated	I.	recitation of spells to produce a magic effect
____ 10.	stupor	J.	an agitated disturbance
____ 11.	elation	K.	to free from evil spirits or malign influences
____ 12.	acrid	L.	unaffected by pleasure or pain; impassive

Vocabulary Worksheets *Bless Me, Ultima*

Chapters 11-12
Part I: Using Prior Knowledge and Context Clues
Below are the sentences in which the vocabulary words appear in the text. Read the sentence. Use any clues you can find in the sentence combined with your prior knowledge, and write what you think the underlined words mean on the lines provided.

1. The huge tail swished and *contemptuously* flipped it aside.

2. I felt weak and powerless in the knowledge of the *impending* doom.

3. It is the sweet water of the moon, my mother *crooned* softly, it is the water the Church chose to make holy and place in its font.

4. There were many things in Ultima's room that I *instinctively* knew I should not touch, but I could not understand why she was so blunt about the dolls.

5. "Why are farmers out playing *vigilantes* when they should be home, sitting before a warm fire, playing cards, counting the rich harvest, eh?"

Part II: Determining the Meaning Match the vocabulary words to their dictionary definitions.

_____ 1. contemptuously   A. those who enforce laws themselves
_____ 2. impending   B. disdainfully; scornfully
_____ 3. crooned   C. done by innate aptitude
_____ 4. instinctively   D. to be about to take place
_____ 5. vigilantes   E. sung softly or in a humming way

Vocabulary Worksheets *Bless Me, Ultima*

Chapters 13-14
Part I: Using Prior Knowledge and Context Clues
Below are the sentences in which the vocabulary words appear in the text. Read the sentence. Use any clues you can find in the sentence combined with your prior knowledge, and write what you think the underlined words mean on the lines provided.

1. He would have to bury his daughter in unholy ground, and without the saving grace of the mass her soul was doomed to *perdition.*

2. "There is if you're a Catholic!" Lloyd *countered*.

3. "I'll give you an A," Miss Violet said in *exasperation.*

4. "How nasty," Lloyd *scoffed*.

5. The door opened and a crack of light *illuminated* Narciso's face.

6. But how could he stop the *intrusion*?

7. The townspeople had killed Lupito at the bridge and *desecrated* the river.

8. A warm, *pulsating* stream of blood wet his jacket and the snow.

Vocabulary Worksheets *Bless Me, Ultima*

9. And the Trementina sisters led the *caravan* over the path and onto our hill.

_____

Part II: Determining the Meaning   Match the vocabulary words to their dictionary definitions.

____ 1. perdition
____ 2. countered
____ 3. exasperation
____ 4. scoffed
____ 5. illuminated
____ 6. intrusion
____ 7. desecrated
____ 8. pulsating
____ 9. caravan

A. expanding and contracting rhythmically
B. loss of the soul; eternal damnation
C. rude or inappropriate entrance
D. anger or impatience
E. a company of travelers journeying together
F. lit up
G. offered in response
H. violated the sacredness of; profaned
I. mocked or treated with derision

Vocabulary Worksheets *Bless Me, Ultima*

Chapters 15-17
Part I: Using Prior Knowledge and Context Clues
Below are the sentences in which the vocabulary words appear in the text. Read the sentence. Use any clues you can find in the sentence combined with your prior knowledge, and write what you think the underlined words mean on the lines provided.

1. "Just this side of Antón Chico," León said *unperturbed*, "we hit a slick spot, solid ice, and we went down the ditch--"

   _____

2. On the morning my father's *disquietude* was proven.

   _____

3. My mother cried when she kissed her sons good-bye, but she was *resigned*.

   _____

4. I wondered if I would ever really know my brothers, or would they remain but *phantoms* of my dreams.

   _____

5. "You are a murderer!" I shouted with *defiance*.

   _____

6. I had listened to Florence's *heresy*, but the God of the church had not hurled his thunder at me.

   _____

Vocabulary Worksheets *Bless Me, Ultima*

Chapters 15-17
Part II: Determining the Meaning   Match the vocabulary words to their dictionary definitions.

____ 1. unperturbed   A. ghosts or an apparitions
____ 2. disquietude   B. bold resistance
____ 3. phantoms   C. worried unease; anxiety
____ 4. resigned   D. dissension from dogma by a believer
____ 5. defiance   E. not disturbed or confused
____ 6. heresy   F. acquiescent; unresistingly accepting

Vocabulary Worksheets *Bless Me, Ultima*

Chapters 18-20

Part I: Using Prior Knowledge and Context Clues

Below are the sentences in which the vocabulary words appear in the text. Read the sentence. Use any clues you can find in the sentence combined with your prior knowledge, and write what you think the underlined words mean on the lines provided.

1. It is the soul that must be saved, because the soul *endures*.

   _____

2. The proud and the meek, the *arrogant* and the humble are all made equal on Ash Wednesday.

   _____

3. All of the saints' statues in the church were covered with purple *sheaths.*

   _____

4. Then *abruptly* my thoughts were scattered.

   _____

5. "Aye, Gabriel Márez," the gray, *emaciated* face smiled weakly, "it does my heart good to see an old compadre, an old vaquero--"

   _____

6. "The imagination!" Téllez laughed *sardonically*.

   _____

7. "The three tortured spirits are not to blame, they are *manipulated* by brujas--"

   _____

Vocabulary Worksheets *Bless Me, Ultima*

Chapters 18-20

Part II: Determining the Meaning Match the vocabulary words to their dictionary definitions.

____ 1. endures
____ 2. arrogant
____ 3. sheaths
____ 4. abruptly
____ 5. emaciated
____ 6. sardonically
____ 7. manipulated

A. suddenly
B. made extremely thin
C. influenced shrewdly or deviously
D. continues in existence; lasts
E. tubular coverings, as used for knife blades
F. scornfully or cynically mocking
G. making claims to unwarranted importance

Vocabulary Worksheets *Bless Me, Ultima*

Chapters 21-22
Part I: Using Prior Knowledge and Context Clues
Below are the sentences in which the vocabulary words appear in the text. Read the sentence. Use any clues you can find in the sentence combined with your prior knowledge, and write what you think the underlined words mean on the lines provided.

1. Seeing him made questions and worries evaporate, and I remained *transfixed*, caught and caressed by the essential elements of sky and earth and water.

   _____

2. "A religion different from the religion of the Lunas," I was again talking to myself, *intrigued* by the easy flow of thoughts and the openness with which I divulged them to my father.

   _____

3. "I came from a people who held the wind as brother, because he is free, and the horse as companion, because he is the living, *fleeting* wind . . . . "

   _____

4. When I heard that the hair on my back *bristled*.

   _____

5. "We *indebted* ourselves to her when she saved our brother, a debt I will gladly pay."

   _____

6. The sharp, reverberating hoof beats that moments ago had mixed into the *surging* sound of the river were now a crescendo upon me.

   _____

7. That sympathy for people my father said she possessed had overcome all *obstacles*.

   _____

Vocabulary Worksheets *Bless Me, Ultima*

8. I was about to shout and answer that I was here and well when I saw the *lurking* shadow under the juniper tree.

_____

Part II: Determining the Meaning   Match the vocabulary words to their dictionary definitions.

_____ 1. transfixed
_____ 2. divulged
_____ 3. fleeting
_____ 4. bristled
_____ 5. indebted
_____ 6. reverberating
_____ 7. obstacles
_____ 8. lurking

A. made known (something private or secret)
B. caused to stand erect; stiffened
C. resounding in a succession of echoes
D. things that oppose, or stand in the way of
E. lying in wait, as in ambush
F. rendered motionless with terror or amazement
G. morally, socially, or legally obligated to another
H. moving swiftly; rapid or nimble

ANSWER KEY VOCABULARY
Bless Me, Ultima

Chapters 1-3
Uno-Tres
1. G
2. B
3. J
4. D
5. I
6. F
7. A
8. C
9. H
10. E
11. K
12. L

Chapters 4-8
Cuatro-Ocho
1. I
2. H
3. B
4. G
5. A
6. F
7. C
8. J
9. E
10. D

Chapters 9-10
Nueve-Diez
1. J
2. E
3. B
4. L
5. K
6. A
7. I
8. D
9. G
10. C
11. H
12. F

Chapters 11-12
Once-Doce
1. B
2. D
3. E
4. C
5. A

Chapters 13-14
Trece-Catorce
1. B
2. G
3. D
4. I
5. F
6. C
7. H
8. A
9. E

Chapters 15-17
Quince-Diecisiete
1. E
2. C
3. A
4. F
5. B
6. D

Chapters 18-20
Dieciocho-Veinte
1. D
2. G
3. E
4. A
5. B
6. F
7. C

Chapters 21-22
Veintiuno-Veintidós
1. F
2. A
3. H
4. B
5. G
6. C
7. D
8. E

SPANISH TERMS AND PHRASES
This is for information only, and will not be tested.

llano, p. 1: flat, level ground

curandera, p. 2: a woman who uses herbs and ancient remedies to heal the sick

"Está sola, ya no queda gente en el pueblito de Las Pasturas." p. 2: She is alone, there are not people in the village of Las Pasturas---

vaquero. p. 2 cowherd, herdsman

tejanos, p. 2 Texans

"Qué lastima," p. 2: What a shame.

sala, p. 2: the living room, parlor

"Es verdad," p. 3: It's true.

brujas, p. 4: witches

"Está bien," p. 4: That's good

conquistadores, p. 6 conquerors

molino, p. 7: mill

atole, p. 7: cornflour gruel

"Jasón no está aquí," p. 10: Jason is not here.

"¿Dónde está?", p. 10" Where is he?

"Madre de Dios,", p. 11: Mother of God

"Buenas días te de Dios, a ti y a tu familia." p. 11: Good day to God, to you, and your family.

"Pase, Grande, pase. Nuestra casa es su casa," p. 12: Pass (come in), Grande. Our house is your house.

cuentos, p. 13: stories

andale, p. 15: come, walk

"Un momento," p. 15: just a minute

"Mataron a mi hermano," p. 15 My brother has been killed/murdered.

"Ya vengo," p. 15: I'm coming already

aviso, p. 15: information, announcement

"Chávez, ¿Qué pasa?" p. 16: Chavez, what happened, what's going on?

"¿Pero, qué dices, hombre?" p. 16: But, who says this, man?

"Lo mató, lo mató." p.16: He's murdered, he's dead.

bosque, p. 17: forest

la llorona, p. 26: weeper, mourner

Y las campanas de la iglesia están doblando. . . , P. 31: And the church bells were tolling. . .

Por la sangre de Lupito, todos debemos de rogar,
Que Dios la saque de pena y la lleve a descansar . . . , p. 32: For the blood of Lupito, all must pray That God remove the sorrow and take him to rest.

"Ven acá," p. 32: come here.

"Es una mujer que no ha pecado . . . " p. 33: It is a woman who has not sinned.

"Hechicera, bruja," p. 33: enchanter, witch
¡
una mujer con un deinte, que llama a toda la gente, p. 34: a woman with a tooth, who calls all the people

Arrímense vivos y difuntos, aquí estamos todos juntos, p. 35: They approach alive and deceased Here we are all together.

'¡Mira! Qué suerte, tunas!" p. 40: Look, what luck, prickly pears.

manzanilla, p. 42: chamomile

mollera, p. 42: crown, top of the head

muy sabrosos, p. 42: very delicious

"Cabritos, Cabroncitos!" p. 43: kids, little kids (baby goats)

ristras, p. 49: wreaths made from dried red chiles, used as decorations in and on houses

¡Ay, Dios, otro día!" p. 51: Oh, God, another day!

mujer, p. 51: woman

¿Cómo te llamas? p. 57: What is your name?

la triesta de la vida, p. 59: the sadness of life

¡Cuidado! ¡Saludos a papá y a todos! ¡Adiós! p. 90: Take care. Greetings to papa and all. Good-bye.
¡Toma! p. 93: Take it!

vieja, p. 93: old woman

mantas, p. 95: shawls

"Gracias por mi vida," p. 104: Thank you for my life.

¿Quién es? p. 129: Who is it?

¿Qué pasa aquí? p. 132: What's going on here?

mitote, p. 138: riot, uproar

"Que Dios te bendiga." p. 149: May God bless you.

"¡Te voy a matar, cabrón!" p. 160: I'm going to kill you, goat!

p. 161: These words are curses and epithets.

"¡Ay que diablo!" p. 162: Ay, what a devil!

"¡Sangre!" p. 171: blood

pesadilla, p. 172: nightmare

bizcochitos, p. 178: little biscuits

jefa, jefe, p. 180: chief (female, male)

entremetido, p. 188: meddler, intruder

"voy a tirar tripas," p. 206: I'm going to throw up.

"¡Gracias a Dios que venites!" p. 229: Thanks to God who comes!

acequia, p. 250: canal, trench

grillos, p. 256: crickets

"Espíritu de mi alma!" Spirit of my soul!

DAILY LESSON PLANS

LESSON ONE

<u>Objectives</u>
1. To introduce the *Bless Me, Ultima* unit
2. To relate students' prior knowledge to the new material
3. To distribute books and other related materials
4. To do the prereading work for Chapters 1-3 (Uno-Tres)

<u>Activity #1</u>

Show a map of New Mexico. Have some pictures of the area and the Mexican-Americans who live there. Locate the towns of Pastura (Las Pasturas) and Puerto de Luna (El Puerto de la Luna) and Guadalupe county. Explain that this is the setting of the novel. You may want to play some traditional Mexican-American music to get students in the mood for reading the novel. Give students some background about the Mexican-American settlement of New Mexico, including the following: New Mexico was originally inhabited by the Navajo, Pueblo, and Apache tribes. It was next settled by Spaniards and Mexicans who migrated from Mexico. New Mexico was ceded to the United States in 1848. It is the 47th state, admitted in 1912. The official languages are Spanish and English.

<u>Activity #2</u>

Invite students to think back to what they were like when they were seven years old. Have them discuss what they were like, what they thought about, and what they did. Ask if they thought about topics such as good vs. evil, a struggle with religious beliefs, and choosing a way of life. Tell them Antonio, the central character, thinks about all of these.

<u>Activity #3</u>

Ask what students think the title could be referring to. Do a group KWL sheet with the students (form included.) Put any information the students know in the K column (What I Know.) Ask students what they want to find out and put that information in the W column (What I Want to Find Out.) Keep the sheet and refer back to it after reading the novel, and complete the L column (What I Learned.)

<u>Activity #4</u>

Distribute the materials students will use in this unit. Explain in detail how students are to use these materials.

<u>Study Guides</u> Students should preview the study guide questions before each reading assignment to get a feeling for what events and ideas are important in that section. After reading the section, students will (as a class or individually) answer the questions to review the important events and ideas from that section of the book. Students should keep the study guides as study materials for the unit test.

Reading Assignment Sheet You need to fill in the reading assignment sheet to let students know when their reading has to be completed. You can either write the assignment sheet on a side blackboard or bulletin board and leave it there for students to see each day, or you can "ditto" copies for each student to have. In either case, you should advise students to become very familiar with the reading assignments so they know what is expected of them.

Extra Activities Center The Unit Resource portion of this unit contains suggestions for a library of related books and articles in your classroom as well as crossword and word search puzzles. Make an extra activities center in your room where you will keep these materials for students to use. (Bring the books and articles in from the library and keep several copies of the puzzles on hand.) Explain to students that these materials are available for students to use when they finish reading assignments or other class work early.

Books Each school has its own rules and regulations regarding student use of school books. Advise students of the procedures that are normal for your school.

Activity #5
Show students how to preview the study questions and do the vocabulary work for Chapters 1-3 of *Bless Me, Ultima*. If students do not finish this assignment in class, they should complete it prior to the next class meeting.

NOTE: Throughout the novel there are descriptions of Antonio's dreams. Read these aloud to students as they close their eyes and try to visualize the dreams. There are also several words and phrases in Spanish. A glossary and translation is included in the Pre-Reading vocabulary section of this Unit Plan. Invite students who speak Spanish to read these passages aloud to the class.

KWL LESSON ONE *Bless Me, Ultima*

Directions: Before reading, think about what you already know about Rudolfo Anaya and/or *Bless Me, Ultima*. Write the information in the K column. Think about what you would like to find out from reading the book. Write your questions in the W column. After you have read the book, use the L column to write the answers to your questions from the W column, and anything else you remember from the book.

K What I Know	W What I Want to Find Out	L What I Learned

LESSON TWO

Objectives
1. To read Chapters 1-3 (Uno-Tres)
2. To review the main ideas and events from Chapters 1-3
3. To introduce the Nonfiction assignment

Activity #1
You may want to read Chapter 1 aloud to the students to set the mood for the novel. Invite willing students to read Chapters 2-3 aloud to the rest of the class.

Activity #2
Give the students time to answer the study guide questions, and then discuss the answers in detail. Write the answers on the board or overhead projector so students can have the correct answers for study purposes. Encourage students to take notes. If the students own their books, encourage them to use highlighter pens to mark important passages and the answers to the study guide questions.

Note: It is a good practice in public speaking and leadership skills for individuals students to take charge of leading the discussion of the study questions. Perhaps a different student could go to the front of the class and lead the discussion each day that the study questions are discussed during this unit. Of course, the teacher should guide the discussion when appropriate and be sure to fill in any gaps the students leave.

Activity #3
Distribute copies of the Nonfiction Assignment sheet and go over it in detail with the students. Give them the due date for the assignment (Lesson 18.) Encourage them to focus on topics that are relevant to the novel. Some possible topics are: The geographical features of New Mexico and their influence on the way of life there; the early Spanish-Mexican settlement of the area; the influence of the Catholic Church on the Mexican-American way of life; other Mexican-American writers; the role of the curandera in Mexican-American society, past and present; living in a bi-cultural society; and the effects of the explosion of the first atomic bomb in Alamogordo, New Mexico (White Sands Proving Grounds.)

NONFICTION ASSIGNMENT SHEET *Bless Me, Ultima*
(To be completed after reading the required nonfiction article)

Name _____ Date _____ Class _____

Title of Nonfiction Read _____

Written By _____ Publication Date _____

I. Factual Summary: Write a short summary of the piece you read.

II. Vocabulary:
   1. With which vocabulary words in the piece did you encounter some degree of difficulty?

   2. How did you resolve your lack of understanding with these words?

III. Interpretation: What was the main point the author wanted you to get from reading his/her work?

IV. Criticism:
   1. With which points of the piece did you agree or find easy to accept? Why?

   2. With which points of the piece did you disagree or find difficult to believe? Why?

V. Personal Response: What do you think about this piece? OR How does this piece influence your ideas?

LESSON THREE

Objectives
1. To do the prereading and vocabulary work for chapters 4-8 (Cuatro-Ocho)
2. To read chapters 4-8
3. To give students practice reading orally
4. To evaluate students' oral reading

Activity #1
Give students about fifteen minutes to preview the study questions for chapters 4-8 and do the related vocabulary work.

Activity #2
Have students read chapters 4-8 of *Bless Me, Ultima* out loud in class. You probably know the best way to get readers with your class; pick students at random, ask for volunteers, or use whatever method works best for your group. If you have not yet completed an oral reading evaluation for your students for this marking period, this would be a good opportunity to do so. A form is included with this unit for your convenience.

If students do not complete reading Chapters 4-8 in class, they should do so prior to your next class meeting.

LESSON FOUR

Objectives
1. To check students' understanding of the main ideas and events from Chapters 1-8 (Uno-Ocho)
2. To introduce PROJECT STORYTELLER, a project that goes along with this unit
3. To preview the study questions for Chapters 9-10 (Nueve-Diez)
4. To familiarize students with the vocabulary in Chapters 9-10
5. To read Chapters 9-10

Activity #1
Quiz--distribute quizzes (multiple choice study questions for Chapters 1-8) and give students about ten minutes to complete them. Have students exchange papers. Grade the quizzes as a class. Collect the papers for recording the grades.

Activity #2
If you have decided not do Project Storyteller with your students during this unit (instead of after it,) take time now to explain what the project is and how the students will do it. (See the information following this lesson for guidelines.)

Activity #3
      Give students about fifteen minutes to preview the study questions for Chapters 9-10 and do the related vocabulary work.

Activity #4
      Have students read Chapters 9-10 for the rest of the period. If you have not completed the oral reading evaluations, do so now. If the evaluations have been completed, you may want the students to read silently. If students do not complete the reading assignment in class, they should do so prior to your next class meeting.

PROJECT STORYTELLER *Bless Me, Ultima*

Objectives

Project Storyteller is a total class project for use in conjunction with the novel *Bless Me, Ultima*. Rudolfo Anaya successfully weaves the *cuentos*, or stories and legends of the Mexican-American people throughout the book, thus preserving their native culture in a multi-cultural society. This is a good opportunity to have students research their own cultural backgrounds and discover their own rich heritage through folktales and legends.

THE PROJECT

This project is separate from the rest of the *Bless Me, Ultima* unit so you can either use it while you are doing the *Bless Me, Ultima* unit or as a separate mini-unit after you have completed the unit test for the book. Also, having it as a separate project enables you to eliminate it if you want to or need to for some reason, without disrupting the flow of the unit.

Grading Distribute your grading policy along with the other information about the project. One possibility is to give two grades, one for research and one for the storytelling delivery. The actual assigning of point values is up to you.

Assignment 1 Invite a storyteller to come to the class. Ask the storyteller to tell stories and also tell how he/she conducts research, finds sources and prepares for the actual storytelling. Suggest that students prepare questions ahead of time for the storyteller. If possible, give the questions to the storyteller a few days in advance. The public library or a bookstore will probably have information about the local chapter of the National Storytellers' Association. The drama department of a college or university may also be able to put you in contact with a storyteller. If you are not able to arrange for a guest to come in, use a storytelling audio or video tape, available in most public libraries.

Assignment 2 Have students do independent research on their own cultural heritage. Suggest possible sources such as family members, friends, the library, local cultural or historical societies, the Internet and foreign language teachers. Some foreign embassies may also be able to provide information. If students cannot find information on their own native cultures, let them choose another culture to research.

Assignment 3 After students have found a few old stories or legends, have them choose one to tell to the class. The presentation should take between five and ten minutes. Have them turn in the name and national origin of the tale. Check them to avoid overlap.

Assignment 4 If possible, give students time in class to practice their storytelling techniques. Offer suggestions as necessary. Students may want to practice with one or two others, so they can critique each other. Encourage students to use props such as costumes and artifacts .

Assignment 5 Set up a schedule for student to present the stories to the class. Use the method that works best for you. Do all presentations in one day or have a few each day for several days. You may want to group presentation so that all stories from one culture are presented on the same day or one after the other. Allow students to video tape the presentations if the so desire.

Assignment 6 Take your storytelling troupe on the road! Arrange to visit an elementary school, daycare center, or senior center. Offer to perform for a school event or PTA or faculty meeting.

Assignment 7 Have each student turn in a written copy of his/her folktale. Bind them together and make a class book for pleasure reading and future reference.

ORAL READING EVALUATION *Bless Me, Ultima*

Name_____Class_____Date_____

SKILL	EXCELLENT	GOOD	AVERAGE	FAIR	POOR
Fluency	5	4	3	2	1
Clarity	5	4	3	2	1
Audibility	5	4	3	2	1
Pronunciation	5	4	3	2	1
_____	5	4	3	2	1
_____	5	4	3	2	1

Total _____ Grade _____

Comments:

LESSON FIVE

Objectives
1. To give students the opportunity to practice writing to persuade
2. To give the teacher the opportunity to evaluate each student's writing skills

Activity #1
Distribute Writing Assignment #1 and discuss the directions in detail. Allow the remaining class time for students to work on the assignment. Give students an additional two or three days to complete the assignment, if necessary.

NOTE: If you have students who, for whatever reason, are not able to research their own family, allow them to complete the project using a friend's family. Or, they could read a biography or autobiography of a famous person and complete the assignment based on that person's family.

Activity #2
Distribute copies of the Writing Evaluation Form (included in this Unit Plan.) Explain to students that during Lesson Nine you will be holding individual writing conferences about this writing assignment. Make sure they are familiar with the criteria on the Writing Evaluation Form.

Follow-Up: After you have graded the assignments, have a writing conference with each student, (This unit schedules one in Lesson Nine.) After the writing conference, allow students to revise their papers using your suggestions to complete the revision. I suggest grading the revisions on an A-C-E scale (all revisions well-done, some revisions made, few or no revisions made.) This will speed your grading time and still give some credit for the students' efforts.

LESSON SIX

Objectives
1. To review the main ideas and events in Chapters 9-10 (Nueve-Diez)
2. To preview the study questions and vocabulary for Chapters 11-12 (Once-Doce)
3. To read Chapters 11-12 silently

Activity #1
Ask students to get out their books and some paper (not their study guides.) Tell them to write down ten questions and answers which cover the main events and ideas in Chapters 9-10. Discuss the students' questions and answers orally, making a list on the board of the questions with brief responses. Put a star next to students' questions and answers that are essentially the same as the study guide questions. Be sure that all of the study guide questions are answered.

Activity #2
Give students about fifteen minutes to do the prereading and vocabulary work for Chapters 11-12.

Activity #3
Give students the remainder of the period to begin silently reading Chapters 11-12. Remind them that the reading must be completed prior to your next class meeting.

WRITING ASSIGNMENT #1 *Bless Me, Ultima*

PROMPT

One of the main conflicts in the story is between the Luna and Márez ways of life. Antonio knows a lot about his family background from listening to Ultima and his parents. Your assignment is to find out more about your family background, or genealogy. Go as far back in your family as you are able. You will display this information in the form of a family tree, and with a more in-depth report about one family member.

PREWRITING

The first thing you need to do is think about how to approach the research phase of your assignment. If you want to get information from relatives, which ones will you ask? Will you write them or interview them in person or over the telephone? Are there any other sources of information besides relatives? Then, make appointments with the people you have chosen. Ask their permission if you want to tape record the conversations.

Next, make a list of questions you want to ask. Make enough copies of your list so that you have one for each person being interviewed.

When you have finished your interviews, divide the information into two parts, one for each side of your family. You will use all of this for the family tree. Then choose one family member for your in-depth written report.

DRAFTING-Family Tree

Make a rough draft of your family tree. Check the information against your notes for accuracy. Decide on the size and presentation of your final project. Will you use poster board, make a mobile, or try another creative approach? Make sure to check with your teacher first if you want to do anything unusual. Then make your display.

DRAFTING- In-depth Report

Write about your interesting family member. In the introductory paragraph, give his/her full name and dates of birth and death. Tell how the person is related to you. In the body of the paper, tell the story about the person. Make sure to include names of other people involved, the dates when the event or events took place, and the location. In your closing paragraph, tell why this person interested you, and how you have been influenced by the story or the actual person. Tell how you are similar to, and different from, this relative.

PROOFREADING

When you finish the rough draft of your paper, ask another student to read it. After reading your rough draft, he/she should tell you what he/she liked best about your work, which parts were difficult to understand, and ways in which your work could be improved. Reread your paper considering your critic's comments, and make the corrections you think are necessary.

WRITING EVALUATION FORM *Bless Me, Ultima*

Name _____ Date _____ Class _____

Writing Assignment #1 for *Bless Me, Ultima*

Circle One For Each Item:

In-Depth Report about a Family Member

Introduction	excellent	good	fair	poor
Body Paragraphs	excellent	good	fair	poor
Summary	excellent	good	fair	poor
Grammar	excellent	good	fair	poor (errors noted)
Spelling	excellent	good	fair	poor (errors noted)
Punctuation	excellent	good	fair	poor (errors noted)
Legibility	excellent	good	fair	poor (errors noted)

Family Tree Display for Writing Assignment #1

Creativity	excellent	good	fair	poor (errors noted)
Legibility	excellent	good	fair	poor (errors noted)
Completeness	excellent	good	fair	poor (errors noted)

Strengths:

Weaknesses:

Comments/Suggestions:

LESSON SEVEN

Objectives
> 1. To review the main ideas and events from chapters 11-12 (Once-Doce)
> 2. To preview the study questions and vocabulary for chapters 13-14 (Trece-Catorce)
> 3. To read chapters 13-14

Activity #1
> Review the study guide questions and answers for chapters 11-12.

Activity #2
> Give students about fifteen minutes to complete the prereading and vocabulary work for chapters 13-14.

Activity #3
> Depending on the needs of your group, have the students read these chapters orally or silently. Remind them that any reading not completed in class must be finished before the next class meeting.

LESSON EIGHT

Objectives
> 1. To review the main ideas and events from chapters 13-14
> 2. To introduce Writing Assignment #2

Activity #1
> Go over the study guide questions and answers for chapters 13-14.

Activity #2
> Distribute Writing Assignment #2. Discuss the directions in detail and give students ample time to complete the assignment.

LESSON NINE

Objectives
1. To have students revise their first writing assignment papers
2. To work on other assignments independently

Activity #1
Call students to your desk or some other private area to discuss their papers from Writing Assignment #1. Use the completed Writing Evaluation Form as a basis for your critique.

Activity #2
Students should use this period (when they are not conferencing with you) to work on their Nonfiction assignment, or to review the study guide questions they have covered so far.

WRITING ASSIGNMENT #2 *Bless Me, Ultima*

PROMPT
One of the conflicts in the novel is between Gabriel and his older sons-León, Andrés, and Eugenio. Gabriel wants them to move to California with him. They want to go their own ways and live their own lives. Your assignment is to take the position of either Gabriel or the boys, and argue for your position.

PREWRITING
To begin, decide which side you want to take-Gabriel's or the boys'. On a piece of paper, jot down the main points for your position. Decide which of your points are the strongest and which are the weakest. Organize your points from weakest to strongest and jot down anything you can think of which will support or explain your points.

DRAFTING
Begin with an introductory paragraph in which you introduce your opponent (Gabriel or his sons) to your side of the argument. Follow that with one paragraph for each of the main points you have to support your position. Fill in each paragraph with examples and facts which support your main point. Then, write a paragraph in which you make your final closing statements.

PROMPT
When you finish the rough draft of your paper, ask another student to read it. After reading your rough draft, he/she should tell you what he/she liked best about your work, which parts were difficult to understand, and ways in which your work could be improved. Reread your paper considering your critic's comments, and make the corrections you think are necessary.

PROOFREADING
Do a final proofreading of your paper double-checking your grammar, spelling, organization, and the clarity of your ideas.

LESSON TEN

Objectives
    1. To check to see that students have done the required reading
    1. To complete the prereading and vocabulary work for chapters 15-17
       (Quince- Diecisiete)
    2. To silently read chapters 15-17

Activity #1
    Give students a quiz on chapters 9-14. Use either the short answer or multiple choice form of the study guide questions as a quiz so that in discussing the answers to the quiz you also answer the study guide questions. Collect the papers for grading.

Activity #2
    Give students about fifteen minutes to preview the study questions and do the related vocabulary work.

Activity #3
    Have students read the chapters silently and answer the study guide questions.

LESSON ELEVEN

Objectives
    1. To review the main ideas and events from chapters 15-17 (Quince-Diecisiete)
    2. To preview the study questions and vocabulary for chapters 18-20 (Dieciocho-Veinte)
    3. To read chapters 18-20

Activity #1
    Review the study guide questions and answers for chapters 15-17.

Activity #2
    Give students about fifteen minutes to complete the prereading and vocabulary work for chapters 18-20.

Activity #3
    Depending on the needs of your group, have the students read these chapters orally or silently. Remind them that any reading not completed in class must be finished before the next class meeting.

LESSON TWELVE

Objectives
  1. To review the main ideas and events from chapters 18-20 (Dieciocho-Veinte)
  2. To preview the study questions and vocabulary for chapters 21-22 (Veintiuno-Veintidós)
  3. To read chapters 21-22

Activity #1
  Review the study guide questions and answers for chapters 18-20. Have students work in small groups and go over their answers. They should refer to the text to verify answers where there are disagreements. When all groups have finished, allow time to answer any remaining questions they have.

Activity #2
  Give students about fifteen minutes to complete the prereading and vocabulary work for chapters 21-22.

Activity #3
  Depending on the needs of your group, have the students read these chapters orally or silently. Remind them that any reading not completed in class must be finished before the next class meeting.

LESSON THIRTEEN

Objectives
  1. To review the main ideas and events from chapters 21-22
  2. To review the study guide questions and answers for the entire novel
  3. To discuss *Bless Me, Ultima* at the interpretive and critical levels

Activity #1
  Review the study guide questions and answers for chapters 21-22.

Activity #2
  Allow time for students to ask any questions they have about the novel and the study guides.

Activity #3
  Depending on time, you may want to start using the Extra Writing Assignments Discussion Questions now. If you want to go into more depth with the novel, complete Lesson Fourteen; otherwise, go on to Lesson Fifteen.

LESSON FOURTEEN

<u>Objective</u>
    To discuss *Bless Me, Ultima* at the interpretive and critical levels

<u>Activity #1</u>
    Choose the questions from the Extra Writing Assignments/Discussion Questions which seem most appropriate for your students. A class discussion of these questions is most effective if students have been given the opportunity to formulate answers to the questions prior to the discussion. To this end, you may either have all the students formulate answers to all the questions, divide the class into groups and assign one or more questions to each group, or you could assign one questions to each student in your class. The option you choose will make a difference in the amount of class time needed for this activity.

<u>Activity #2</u>
    After students have had ample time to formulate answers to the questions, begin your class discussion of the questions and the ideas presented by the questions. Be sure students take note during the discussion so they have information to study for the unit test.

LESSON FIFTEEN

<u>Objectives</u>
    1. To introduce Writing Assignment #3
    2. To give students time to work on the writing assignment

<u>Activity #1</u>
    Distribute copies of Writing Assignment #3. Discuss the directions in detail and give students ample time to complete the assignment.

EXTRA WRITING ASSIGNMENT/ DISCUSSION QUESTIONS
Bless Me, Ultima

Interpretive

1. What are the main conflicts in the story, and how are they resolved?

2. Based on the facts in the story, can you tell approximately in what year the story takes place? Does it matter?

3. Discuss the main themes in the novel.

4. Give a complete character analysis of one of the following: Gabriel, María, Antonio, or Ultima.

5. Discuss the type of family structure portrayed in the novel.

6. Discuss the significance and symbolism of Ultima's owl.

7. Discuss the significance of one of Antonio's dreams.

8. How does the author show Antonio's loss of faith?

9. Discuss the use of emotions in the novel.

10. What is superstition? Give examples of it from the novel.

11. Why did Ultima take Antonio with her when she went to cure people?

12. What is the significance of the three dolls that Ultima held to Lucas's mouth?

13. Why was Ultima so blunt in telling Antonio not to touch the three dolls?

14. Where is the climax of the novel? Justify your answer.

15. Which events in the novel are "turning points" which affect the course of the plot?

16. Why did Ultima tell Antonio to burn all of her things when she died?

17. Discuss the role of religion in the novel.

18. What is foreshadowing? Discuss the use of foreshadowing in the novel.

Critical

19. How does Anaya use the southwestern setting to convey the mood of the novel?

20. Explain the significance of the title *Bless Me, Ultima*.

21. What purpose do the folktales (cuentos) in the story serve?

22. Do any of the characters change in the course of the novel? If so, who, and how?

23. Was the symbolism of the owl effective? Why or why not?

24. How did the use of dreams further the plot and character development in the novel?

25. Describe Anaya's writing style. How does it influence our perception of the story?

26. Who is the main character of the novel? Defend your choice.

27. Is the story of Bless Me, Ultima believable? Why or why not?

28. Does the use of Spanish words and phrases add to or detract from the novel?

29. Is the character of Antonio believable? Would a seven year old child have the kind of thoughts he does?

Personal Response

30. Did you enjoy the novel? Why or why not?

31. Would you rather be like the Luna or the Márez family?

32. Would you recommend this book to a friend?

33. How did you feel about Antonio as a person?

34. What did you learn about the Mexican-American culture of the Southwest from reading the novel?

35. Did you like the ending of the novel? Why or why not?

36. What do you think Antonio meant by the "magic in the letters?"

37. On page 55, Antonio wonders if the power of good and evil was the same. What is your opinion?

38. Have you ever been in a situation like Antonio's in school, when you did not speak the same language as the rest of the class, or for other reasons felt like an outcast? What was it like for you? Did having this experience help you relate to Antonio?

39. How do you think witnessing the murders affected Antonio?

40. What do you think Antonio will do when he grows up? Why?

QUOTATIONS *Bless Me, Ultima*
Discuss the significance of the following quotations.

1. The magical time of childhood stood still, and the pulse of the living earth pressed its mystery into my living blood. She took my hand, and the silent, magic powers she possessed made beauty from the raw, sun-baked llano, the green river valley, and the blue bowl which was the white sun's home.

2. Campos could not keep the animal penned up because somehow the horse was very close to the spirit of the man, and so the horse was allowed to roam free and no vaquero on that llano would throw a lazo on that horse. It was as if someone had died, and they turned their gaze from the spirits that walked the earth.

3. "-She served the people all her life, and now the people are scattered, driven like tumbleweeds by the winds of war. The war sucks everything dry," my father said solemnly, "it takes the young boys overseas, and their families move to California where there is work-"

4. It was the custom to provide for the old and the sick. There was always room in the safety and warmth of la familia for one more person, be that person stranger or friend.

5. Its soft hooting was like a song, and as it grew rhythmic it calmed the moonlit hills and lulled us to sleep. Its song seemed to say that it had come to watch over us.

6. I had been afraid of the awful *presence* of the river, which was the soul of the river, but through her I learned that my spirit shared in the spirit of all things.

7. I do not know if he saw me, or if the light cut off his vision, but I saw his bitter, contorted grin. As long as I live I will never forget those wild eyes, like the eyes of a trapped, savage animal.

8. And where was Lupito's soul winging to, or was it washing down the river to the fertile valley of my uncles' farms?

9. How would I ever wash away the stain of blood from the sweet waters of my river!

10. Why two people as opposite as my father and my mother had married I do not know. Their blood and their ways had kept them at odds, and yet for all this, we were happy.

11. There is a time in the last few days of summer when the ripeness of autumn fills the air, and time is quiet and mellow. I lived that time fully, strangely aware of a new world opening up and taking shape for me.

12. I looked at the three of them standing there, and I felt that I was seeing them for the last time: Ultima in her wisdom, my mother in her dream, and my father in his rebellion.

13. She took me to the front of the room and spoke to the other boys and girls. She pointed at me but I did not understand her. Then the other boys and girls laughed and pointed at me. I did not feel so good. Thereafter I kept away from the groups as much as I could and worked alone. I worked hard. I listened to the strange sounds. I learned new names, new words.

14. We struggled against the feeling of loneliness that gnawed at our souls and we overcame it; that feeling I never shared again with anyone, not even with Horse and Bones, or the Kid and Samuel, or Cico or Jasón.

15. My three brothers were back and our household was complete. My mother cared for them like a mother hen cares for her chicks, even though the hawk of war has flown away. My father was happy and full of life, regenerated by talk of the coming summer and moving to California. And I was busy at school, driven by the desire to make mine the magic of letters and numbers.

16. I got down and put my pants on. It hurt where they had spanked me. I didn't know whether to cry or laugh with them. There was an empty feeling inside, not because they spanked me, but because they would be gone again.

17. "You must understand that when anybody, bruja or curandera, priest or sinner, tampers with the fate of a man that sometimes a chain of events is set into motion over which no one will have ultimate control. You must be willing to accept the responsibility."

18. "That is why they call this place El Puerto de la Luna," she said to me, "because this valley is the door through which the moon of each month passes on its journey from the east to the west-"

19. "¡Ay bruja!" Tenorio threatened with his fist, "for what you have said to shame my daughters and my good name in front of those men, I will see you dead!"

20. The priest at El Puerto did not want the people to place much faith in the powers of la curandera. He wanted the mercy and faith of the church to be the villagers' only guiding light.

21. It seemed that the more I knew about people the more I knew about the strange magic hidden in their hearts.

22. "Why are they like that?" I asked Cico. . . "I don't know," Cico answered, "except that people, grown-ups and kids, seem to want to hurt each other-and it's worse when they're in a group."

23. I felt my body trembling as I saw the bright golden form disappear. I knew I had witnessed a miraculous thing, the appearance of a pagan god, a thing as miraculous as the curing of my Uncle Lucas. And I thought, the power of God failed where Ultima's worked; and then a sudden illumination of beauty and understanding flashed through my mind. This is what I had expected God to do at my first holy communion! If God was witness to my beholding of the golden carp then I had sinned!

24. "Antonio," she said calmly and placed her hand on my shoulder. "I cannot tell you what to believe. Your father and mother can tell you, because you are their blood, but I cannot. As you grow into manhood you must find your own truths-"

25. *The waters are one, Antonio. I looked into her bright, clear eyes and understood her truth. You have been seeing only parts, she finished, and not looking beyond into the great cycle that binds us all.*

26. A faint glitter caught my eye. I bent down and picked up the two needles that had been stuck to the top of the door frame. Whether someone had broken the cross they made, or whether they had fallen, I would never know.

27. The soul was lost, unsafe, unsure, suffering-why couldn't there be a god who would never punish his people, a god who would be forgiving all of the time?

28. "It will only end when blood is spilled," Samuel said. "My father says that the blood of a man thickens with the desire for revenge, and if a man is to be complete again then he must let some of that thick blood flow-"

29. Perhaps when I make my communion I will understand, I thought.

30. A thousand questions pushed through my mind, but the Voice within me did not answer. There was only silence. Perhaps I had not prepared right. I opened my eyes.

31. "You have to choose, Tony," Cico said, "you have to choose between the god of the church, or the beauty that is here and now-"

32. The lonely river was a sad place to be when one is a small boy who has just seen a friend die. And it grew sadder when the bells of the church began to toll, and the afternoon shadows lengthened.

33. "Then maybe I do not have to be just Márez, or Luna, perhaps I can be both-" I said.

34. "Understanding comes with life," he answered, "as a man grows he sees life and death, he is happy and sad, he works, plays, meets people-sometimes it takes a lifetime to acquire understanding, because in the end understanding is simply having a sympathy for people," he said.

35. He cursed and fired. The thundering report of the rifle followed the flash of fire. That shot destroyed the quiet, moonlit peace of the hill, and it shattered my childhood into a thousand fragments that long ago stopped falling and are now dusty relics gathered in distant memories.

36. "I bless you in the name of all that is good and strong and beautiful, Antonio. Always have the strength to live. Love life, and if despair enters your heart, look for me in the evenings when the wind is gentle and the owls sing in the hills. I shall be with you-"

LESSON SIXTEEN

Objectives
1. To give students the opportunity to do research for their Nonfiction Assignment
2. To assist students in the proper use of the school library

Activity

Take your class to the library for the entire class period. Tell them they can have the time to work on their Nonfiction Assignment. Students who have completed the assignment can use the time to read for pleasure.

LESSON SEVENTEEN

Objectives
1. To give students the opportunity to present their stories for Project Storyteller
2. To give student exposure to folk tales and legends from a variety of cultures
3. To allow students to practice good listening skills

Activity

Invite students to tell their stories to the class. You may want to group all stories from the same cultural background together, to give students a more complete understanding of the culture.

LESSON EIGHTEEN

Objectives
1. To widen the breadth of students' knowledge about the topics discussed or touched upon in *Bless Me, Ultima*
2. To check students' non-fiction assignments

Activity

Ask each student to give a brief oral report about the nonfiction work he/she read for the nonfiction assignment. Your criteria for evaluating this report will vary depending on the level of your students. You may wish for students to give a complete report without using notes of any kind, or you may want students to read directly from a written report, or you may want to do something in between these two extremes. Just make students aware of your criteria in ample time for them to prepare their reports.

Start with one student's report, After that, ask if anyone else in the class has read on a topic related to the first student's report. If no one has, choose another student at random. After each report, be sure to ask if anyone has a report related to the one just completed. That will help keep a continuity during the discussion of the reports.

WRITING ASSIGNMENT # 3 *Bless Me, Ultima*

PROMPT

Throughout the story, Ultima is accused of being a witch. Ultima neither admitted to nor denied the accusation. Your assignment is to express your personal opinion about the question. Was Ultima a witch or not?

PREWRITING

Decide on an opinion: Ultima was a witch, or she was not. Reread the chapters from the book that dealt with Ultima curing people or breaking a curse. Look for evidence that supports your view. Take notes from the book, including page numbers.

DRAFTING

Organize your ideas into a rough outline. In the first paragraph, give a little bit of background about the accusations in the story. Then state your opinion. In the next paragraphs, present your arguments . Fill in the paragraphs with details from the story. In the last paragraph, summarize the rest of the paper, and re-state your opinion.

PROMPT

After you have finished a rough draft of your letter, revise it until you are happy with your work. Then ask another student to tell you what he/she likes best about your work, and what things he/she thinks can be improved. Take another look at your letter, keeping in mind your critic's suggestions, and make the revisions you feel are necessary.

PROOFREADING

Do a final proofreading of your paper double-checking your grammar, spelling, organization, and the clarity of your ideas.

LESSON NINETEEN

<u>Objective</u>
To review all of the vocabulary work done in this unit

VOCABULARY REVIEW ACTIVITIES

1. Divide your class into two teams and have an old-fashioned spelling or definition bee.

2. Give each of your students (or students in groups of two, three or four) a *Bless Me, Ultima* Vocabulary Word Search Puzzle. The person (group) to find all of the vocabulary words in the puzzle first wins.

3. Give students a *Bless Me, Ultima* Vocabulary Word Search Puzzle without the word list. The person or group to find the most vocabulary words in the puzzle wins.

4. Use a *Bless Me, Ultima* Vocabulary Crossword Puzzle. Put the puzzle onto a transparency on the overhead projector (so everyone can see it), and do the puzzle together as a class.

5. Give students a *Bless Me, Ultima* Vocabulary Matching Worksheet to do.

6. Divide your class into two teams. Use the *Bless Me, Ultima* vocabulary words with their letters jumbled as a word list. Student 1 from Team A faces off against Student 1 from Team B. You write the first jumbled word on the board. The first student (1A or 1B) to unscramble the word wins the chance for his/her team to score points. If 1A wins the jumble, go to student 2A and give him/her a definition. He/she must give you the correct spelling of the vocabulary word which fits that definition. If he/she does, Team A scores a point, and you give student 3A a definition for which you expect a correctly spelled matching vocabulary word. Continue giving Team A definitions until some team member makes an incorrect response. An incorrect response sends the game back to the jumbled-word face off, this time with students 2A and 2B. Instead of repeating giving definitions to the first few students of each team, continue with the student after the one who gave the last incorrect response on the team. For example, if Team B wins the jumbled-word face-off, and student 5B gave the last incorrect answer for Team B, you would start this round of definition questions with student 6B, and so on. The team with the most points wins!

7. Have students write a story in which they correctly use as many vocabulary words as possible. Have students read their compositions orally. Post the most original compositions on your bulletin board!

LESSON TWENTY

Objective
   To review the main ideas presented in *Bless Me, Ultima*

Activity #1
   Choose one of the review games/activities included in the packet and spend your class period as outlined there.

Activity #2
   Remind students of the date for the Unit Test. Stress the review of the Study Guides and their class notes as a last minute, brush-up review for homework.

REVIEW GAMES / ACTIVITIES

1. Ask the class to make up a unit test for *Bless Me, Ultima*. The test should have 4 sections: multiple choice, true/false, short answer and essay. Students may use 1/2 period to make the test, including a separate answer sheet, and then swap papers and use the other 1/2 class period to take a test a classmate has devised (open book).

2. Take 1/2 period for students to make up true and false questions (including the answers.) Collect the papers and divide the class into two teams. Draw a big tic-tac-toe board on the chalk board. Make one team X and one team O. Ask questions to each side, giving each student one turn. If the question is answered correctly, that student's team's letter (X or O) is placed in the box. If the answer is incorrect, no mark is placed in the box. The object is to get three marks in a row like tic-tac-toe. You may want to keep track of the number of games won for each team.

3. Take 1/2 period for students to make up questions (true/false and short answer). Collect the questions. Divide the class into two teams. You'll alternate asking questions to individual members of teams A & B (like in a spelling bee.) The question keeps going from A to B until it is correctly answered, then a new question is asked. A correct answer does not allow the team to get another question. Correct answers are +2 points; incorrect answers are -1 point.

4. Allow students time to quiz each other (in pairs) from their study guides and class notes.

5. Give students a *Bless Me, Ultima* crossword puzzle to complete.

6. Divide your class into two teams. Use the *Bless Me, Ultima* crossword words with their letters jumbled as a word list. Student 1 from Team A faces off against Student 1 from Team B. You write the first jumbled word on the board. The first student (1A or 1B) to unscramble the word wins the chance for his/her team to score points. If 1A wins the jumble, go to student 2A and give him/her a clue. He/she must give you the correct word which matches that clue. If he/she does, Team A scores a point, and you give student 3A a clue for which you expect another correct response. Continue giving Team A clues until some team member makes an incorrect response. An incorrect response sends the game back to the jumbled-word face off, this time with students 2A and 2B. Instead of repeating giving clues to the first few students of each team, continue with the student after the one who gave the last incorrect response on the team.

7. Take on the persona of "The Answer Person." Allow students to ask any question about the book. Answer the questions, or tell students where to look in the book to find the answer.

8. Students may enjoy playing charades with events from the story. Select a student to start. Give him/her a card with a scene or event from the story. Allow the players to use their books to find the scene being described. The first person to guess each charade performs the next one.

9. Play a categories-type quiz game. (A master is included in this Unit Plan.) Make an overhead transparency of the categories form. Divide the class into teams of three or four players each. Have each team choose a recorder and a banker. Choose a team to go first. That team will choose a category and point amount. Ask the question to the entire class. (Use the Study Guide Quiz and Vocabulary questions.) Give the teams one minute to discuss the answer and write it down. Walk around the room and check the answers. Each team that answers correctly receives the points. (Incorrect answers are not penalized; they just don't receive any points.) Cross out that square on the playing board. Play continues until all squares have been used. The winning team is the one with the most points. You can assign bonus points to any square or squares you choose.

10. Have students complete the last column (What I Learned) of the KWL sheet you distributed in Lesson One. Discuss their answers with the class.

11. Play a picture identification game. Have students draw one scene each from the story. Then have them show their drawings, one at a time, to the rest of the class. The viewers should look through their books to find the scene that is shown in the drawing, then read pertinent passages aloud to the class, or summarize the events surrounding the drawing.

NOTE: If students do not need the extra review, omit this lesson and go on to the test.

QUIZ GAME
Bless Me, Ultima

Chapters 1-3	Chapters 4-8	Chapters 9-12	Chapters 13-17	Chapters 18-20	Chapters 21-22
100	100	100	100	100	100
200	200	200	200	200	200
300	300	300	300	300	300
400	400	400	400	400	400
500	500	500	500	500	500

LESSON TWENTY-ONE

Objective
 To test the students' understanding of the main ideas and themes in *Bless Me, Ultima*

Activity #1
 Distribute the *Bless Me, Ultima* Unit Tests. Go over the instructions in detail and allow the students the entire class period to complete the exam.

Activity #2
 Collect all test papers and assigned books prior to the end of the class period.

NOTES ABOUT THE UNIT TESTS IN THIS UNIT:

There are 5 different unit tests which follow.

There are two short answer tests which are based primarily on facts from the novel. The answer key for short answer unit test 1 follows the student test. The answer key for short answer test 2 follows the student short answer unit test 2.

There is one advanced short answer unit test. It is based on the extra discussion questions. Use the matching key for short answer unit test 2 to check the matching section of the advanced short answer unit test. There is no key for the short answer questions. The answers will be based on the discussions you have had during class.

There are two multiple choice unit tests. Following the two unit tests, you will find an answer sheet on which students should mark their answers. The same answer sheet should be used for both tests; however, students' answers will be different for each test. Following the students' answer sheet for the multiple choice tests you will find your answer keys.

The short answer tests have a vocabulary section. You should choose 20 of the vocabulary words from this unit, read them orally and have the students write them down. Then, either have students write a definition or use the words in sentences.

UNIT TESTS

SHORT ANSWER UNIT TEST 1 *Bless Me, Ultima*

I. Matching/Identification

____ 1. Antonio Márez y Luna
____ 2. Ultima
____ 3. Luna family
____ 4. Tenorio
____ 5. Márez family
____ 6. Narciso
____ 7. Gabriel
____ 8. Florence
____ 9. Samuel
____ 10. Cico

A. farmers, knew the secrets of the earth
B. was killed trying to warn Ultima of danger
C. believed he had no sins to confess
D. thought a lot about good vs. evil
E. told Antonio about the golden carp
F. restless, like the sea
G. wanted to move to California
H. sought revenge on Ultima
I. la curandera
J. took Antonio to see the golden carp

II. Short Answer

1. Describe the following people: Antonio, Gabriel, Tenorio, Ultima, and Narciso.

2. What was the conflict between Gabriel and María concerning Antonio's future?

Short Answer Unit Test 1 *Bless Me, Ultima*

3. How did Antonio describe the time spent in El Puerto?

4. What was the conflict between the Márez boys and their parents, and how was it finally resolved?

5. Briefly retell Samuel's story of the carp, including the golden carp.

6. Describe Tenorio's first confrontation with Ultima at the Márez home.

Short Answer Unit Test 1 *Bless Me, Ultima*

7. Describe the fight between Tenorio and Narciso that Antonio witnessed.

8. What did María tell Antonio would happen when he made his first holy communion, and what really happened?

9. Describe the events that happened when Antonio was on his way to church for his first confession.

10. Summarize the events that led up to Ultima's death.

Short Answer Unit Test 1 *Bless Me, Ultima*

III. Essay
Discuss the main themes in the novel.

Short Answer Unit Test 1 *Bless Me, Ultima*

IV. Vocabulary

Listen to the vocabulary words and spell them. After you have spelled all the words, go back and write down the definitions.

	WORD	**DEFINITION**
1.		
2.		
3.		
4.		
5.		
6.		
7.		
8.		
9.		
10.		
11.		
12.		
13.		
14.		
15.		
16.		
17.		
18.		
19.		
20.		

ANSWER KEY SHORT ANSWER UNIT TEST 1 *Bless Me, Ultima*

I. Matching/Identification

D	1.	Antonio Márez y Luna	A.	farmers, knew the secrets of the earth
I	2.	Ultima	B.	was killed trying to warn Ultima of danger
A	3.	Luna family	C.	believed he had no sins to confess
H	4.	Tenorio	D.	thought a lot about good vs. evil
F	5.	Márez family	E.	told Antonio about the golden carp
B	6.	Narciso	F.	restless, like the sea
G	7.	Gabriel	G.	wanted to move to California
C	8.	Florence	H.	sought revenge on Ultima
E	9.	Samuel	I.	la curandera
J	10.	Cico	J.	took Antonio to see the golden carp

II. Short Answer

1. What is the setting of the novel?
    The novel is mainly set in Guadalupe, New Mexico. The nearby towns of las Pasturas and   el Puerto de la Luna are also featured.

2. What was the conflict between Gabriel and María concerning Antonio's future?
    Gabriel wanted Antonio to become a vaquero and live on the llano like the Márez family. María hoped he would become a priest, because there had not been a priest in the Luna family for several generations.

3. How did Antonio describe the time spent in El Puerto?
    He said they enjoyed the time there. It was a happy place where people worked together and helped each other.

4. What was the conflict between the Márez boys and their parents, and how was it finally resolved?
    The boys wanted to move away from home. The parents wanted them to stay in Guadalupe and find work. Gabriel was still holding onto his dream of going with them to California, but the boys told him they would not go. Eventually all three of the boys left home together.

5. Briefly retell Samuel's story of the carp, including the golden carp.
    The townspeople believed it was bad luck to eat the brown carp. According to an old Indian legend, a group known as the people settled in the area, and their gods told them not to eat the carp. After a long drought and famine, they ate the carp, which angered the gods. Most of the gods wanted to kill the people, but one kind god suggested they all be turned into carp. He then asked to be turned into a carp so that he could protect the people. He became the golden carp, the protector of the waters.

6. Describe Tenorio's first confrontation with Ultima at the Márez home.

   Tenorio's daughter died. Tenorio blamed Ultima, and accused her of being a witch, and of killing his daughter. He was coming to kill her in revenge. Narciso came to warn her. He and Gabriel met the mob at the front door. Narciso asked them why farmers were out playing vigilantes when they should be home working and relaxing. He also told them they did not need the darkness to hide their deeds. They were ashamed that the town drunk had pointed out their lowly deeds. Narciso suggested that they give Ultima the test for being a witch.

   (A witch could not walk through a doorway that had a cross on it.) Ultima walked through the door, and therefore passed the test. In the meantime, Ultima's owl scratched out one of Tenorio's eyes. The mob left, but Tenorio was still cursing Ultima. After the men had gone, Antonio found the two needles that had been used to make the cross on the door frame lying on the ground.

7. Describe the fight between Tenorio and Narciso that Antonio witnessed.

   Antonio saw Tenorio and Narciso fighting as they came out of the bar? The bartender and a few other men pulled them apart, and they both left the area. Narciso started out for the Márez home to warn Ultima that Tenorio was again going to try and kill her, because his second daughter was dying. Narciso went to Rosie's to get help from Andrew, but Andrew refused to go with him. Narciso had Tenorio had a confrontation at the juniper tree near the Márez home, which Antonio witnessed. Tenorio shot Narciso, and threatened Antonio. Narciso asked Antonio to hear his confession, and then he died. Antonio ran home to get help.

8. What did María tell Antonio would happen when he made his first holy communion, and what really happened?

   She said he would hold God in his mouth, his body, and his soul. Antonio would speak to God, and God would answer. In reality, Antonio was disillusioned. He felt that he never got the answers from God that he was seeking. The host felt sticky, and the only things he felt were hunger and emptiness.

9. Describe the events that happened when Antonio was on his way to church for his first confession.

   The other boys forced him to hear their confessions. When Florence refused to go the confession and said he didn't have any sins, the other boys got angry. Antonio defended Florence, and the boys turned on him. Horse jumped on his chest while the other boys held Antonio down and hit him. They let him go when they heard the priest calling from the steps of the church.

10. Summarize the events that led up to Ultima's death.

    During the summer, Tenorio's daughter died. Tenorio stretched her body out on the bar of his saloon. Then he got drunk and yelled about getting revenge on Ultima. When the Luna uncles heard of this, they got ready to help Ultima. Pedro said he would take Antonio and drive to Guadalupe to warn Ultima as soon as they were finished in the fields. While walking back to his Grandfather's house, Antonio met Tenorio, who was drunk and on horseback. Tenorio tried to run him down. Antonio evaded him, got scared, and started running back to Guadalupe to warn Ultima. Just as Antonio reached his home, he saw Tenorio hiding near the juniper tree. Tenorio shot and killed the owl. Then Pedro shot Tenorio and killed him. Antonio realized that the owl was her spirit. When he went in the house, he found Ultima in bed, dying. She asked him to bury the owl's body and bury it under a certain forked juniper tree. She also asked him to clean out her room the following day and burn all of her medicine and herbs near the river. He did everything just as she requested.

SHORT ANSWER UNIT TEST 2 *Bless Me, Ultima*

I. Matching/ Identification

____ 1. Tenorio
____ 2. Cico
____ 3. Antonio Márez y Luna
____ 4. Samuel
____ 5. Márez family
____ 6. Florence
____ 7. Narciso
____ 8. Gabriel
____ 9. Ultima
____ 10. Luna family

A. la curandera
B. farmers, knew the secrets of the earth
C. told Antonio about the golden carp
D. took Antonio to see the golden carp
E. wanted to move to California
F. believed he had no sins to confess
G. sought revenge on Ultima
H. was killed trying to warn Ultima of danger
I. restless, like the sea
J. thought a lot about good vs. evil

II. Short Answer

1. What was the conflict between Gabriel and María concerning Antonio's future?

2. Describe the incident with Chávez.

Short Answer Unit Test 2 *Bless Me, Ultima*

3. What did Antonio discover about his cultural background on his first day of school?

4. What was the conflict between the Márez boys and their parents, and how was it resolved?

5. Antonio asked Andrew if he (Andrew) would become a farmer or a priest. What was Andrew's reply?

6. Describe the way Ultima cured Lucas.

Short Answer Unit Test 2 *Bless Me, Ultima*

7. Describe the events that led up to Ultima's death.

8. What did Antonio do every weekend after Easter, and what was the result?

9. What did Cico tell Antonio about God/gods, and about Antonio's choice?

10. Describe Tenorio's first confrontation with Ultima at the Márez home.

Short Answer Unit Test 2 *Bless Me, Ultima*

III. Essay Describe one of Antonio's dreams and its significance.

Short Answer Unit Test 2 *Bless Me, Ultima*

IV. Vocabulary

Listen to the vocabulary words and spell them. After you have spelled all the words, go back and write down the definitions.

WORD	**DEFINITION**
1.	
2.	
3.	
4.	
5.	
6.	
7.	
8.	
9.	
10.	
11.	
12.	
13.	
14.	
15.	
16.	
17.	
18.	
19.	
20.	

ANSWER KEY SHORT ANSWER UNIT TEST 2 *Bless Me, Ultima*

I. Matching/ Identification

G	1.	Tenorio	A.	la curandera
D	2.	Cico	B.	farmers, knew the secrets of the earth
J	3.	Antonio Márez y Luna	C.	told Antonio about the golden carp
C	4.	Samuel	D.	took Antonio to see the golden carp
I	5.	Márez family	E.	wanted to move to California
F	6.	Florence	F.	believed he had no sins to confess
H	7.	Narciso	G.	sought revenge on Ultima
E	8.	Gabriel	H.	was killed trying to warn Ultima of danger
A	9.	Ultima	I.	restless, like the sea
B	10.	Luna family	J.	thought a lot about good vs. evil

<u>II. Short Answer</u>

1. What was the conflict between Gabriel and María concerning Antonio's future?
    Gabriel wanted Antonio to become a vaquero and live on the llano like the Márez family. María hoped he would become a priest, because there had not been a priest in the Luna family for several generations.

2. Describe the incident with Chávez.
    Chávez came to the Márez home, shouting that his brother had been murdered. He asked Gabriel to go with him to search for the murderer, Lupito. Chávez, Gabriel, and other men from the town found Lupito near the river. Narciso tried to reason with him, but the other men shot and killed him.

3. What did Antonio discover about his cultural background on his first day of school?
    He discovered that most of the other students only spoke English. Since he spoke only Spanish, he could not communicate with them. The other students laughed at his traditional Mexican-style lunch. He felt lonely, and found solace with a few other Mexican-American boys. The group overcame their feelings of loneliness and felt a sense of belonging with each other.

4. What was the conflict between the Márez boys and their parents, and how was it resolved?
    The boys wanted to move away from home. The parents wanted them to stay in Guadalupe and work. Gabriel was still holding onto the dream that they would go to California with him. The boys finally left home,

5. Antonio asked Andrew if he (Andrew) would become a farmer or a priest. What was Andrew's reply?
    Andrew said he and his brothers would not become farmers or priests. He thought the war had made them grow up too fast, or they just didn't want to live out their parents' dreams. He told Antonio that he would have to be the one to fit into their parents' dreams.

6. Describe the way Ultima cured Lucas.
    She took Antonio with her. First, she went to the saloon to confront Tenorio. She told him to have his daughters lift the curse, but he refused. Then they returned to Lucas's house. They bathed Lucas. Ultima fed him a remedy of kerosene, herbs, and roots. Antonio felt the spasms of his uncle, and shared the struggle against evil with him. Ultima gave Lucas two other liquid remedies. Then she made three clay dolls, dipped them in wax, and dressed them as women. She held the dolls to Lucas's mouth, then stuck a pin in each doll. Ultima then gave Lucas another remedy to drink. After a while, Lucas vomited a hair ball, and then he was cured. Ultima took all of the cloths she had used, and the hairball, and burned them by the tree where the witches did their dance.

7. Describe the events that led up to Ultima's death.
    During the summer, Tenorio's daughter died. Tenorio stretched her body out on the bar of his saloon. Then he got drunk and yelled about getting revenge on Ultima. When the Luna uncles heard of this, they got ready to help Ultima. Pedro said he would take Antonio and drive to Guadalupe to warn Ultima as soon as they were finished in the fields. While walking back to his Grandfather's house, Antonio met Tenorio, who was drunk and on horseback. Tenorio tried to run him down. Antonio evaded him, got scared, and started running back to Guadalupe to warn Ultima. Just as Antonio reached his home, he saw Tenorio hiding near the juniper tree. Tenorio shot and killed the owl. Then Pedro shot Tenorio and killed him. Antonio realized that the owl was her spirit. When he went in the house, he found Ultima in bed, dying. She asked him to bury the owl's body and bury it under a certain forked juniper tree. She also asked him to clean out her room the following day and burn all of her medicine and herbs near the river. He did everything just as she requested.

8. What did Antonio do every weekend after Easter, and what was the result?
    He went to confession on Saturday and communion on Sunday. He was still dissatisfied, because the God he looked for was not there.

9. What did Cico tell Antonio about God/gods, and about Antonio's choice?
    He said there were many gods-of beauty, of magic, of gardens and backyards. People searched in the stars and foreign countries to find new ones. Cico said Antonio had to choose between the god of the church and the beauty of the ere and now.

10. Describe Tenorio's first confrontation with Ultima at the Márez home.
    Tenorio's daughter died. Tenorio blamed Ultima, and accused her of being a witch, and of killing his daughter. He was coming to kill her in revenge. Narciso came to warn her. He and Gabriel met the mob at the front door. Narciso asked them why farmers were out playing vigilantes when they should be home working and relaxing. He also told them they did not need the darkness to hide their deeds. They were ashamed that the town drunk had pointed out their lowly deeds. Narciso suggested that they give Ultima the test for being a witch. (A witch could not walk through a doorway that had a cross on it.) Ultima walked through the door, and therefore passed the test. In the meantime, Ultima's

owl scratched out one of Tenorio's eyes. The mob left, but Tenorio was still cursing Ultima. After the crowd had gone, Antonio found the two needles from the cross on the door frame lying on the ground.

ADVANCED SHORT ANSWER UNIT TEST *Bless Me, Ultima*

I. Matching/ Identification

____ 1. Tenorio   A. la curandera
____ 2. Cico   B. farmers, knew the secrets of the earth
____ 3. Antonio Márez y Luna   C. told Antonio about the golden carp
____ 4. Samuel   D. took Antonio to see the golden carp
____ 5. Márez family   E. wanted to move to California
____ 6. Florence   F. believed he had no sins to confess
____ 7. Narciso   G. sought revenge on Ultima
____ 8. Gabriel   H. was killed trying to warn Ultima of danger
____ 9. Ultima   I. restless, like the sea
____ 10. Luna family   J. thought a lot about good vs. evil

II. Short Answer

1. Give a complete character analysis of one of the following: Gabriel, María, Antonio, Ultima, or Narciso.

2. Which events in the novel are "turning points" which affect the course of the plot?

Advanced Short Answer Unit Test *Bless Me, Ultima*

3. Do any of the characters change in the course of the novel? If so, who, and how?

4. Explain one of the main conflicts in the novel. If it was resolved, describe the process.

5. Discuss the significance of one of Antonio's dreams.

Advanced Short Answer Unit Test *Bless Me, Ultima*

III. Quotations

Identify the speaker and discuss the significance of each of the following quotations.

1. We struggled against the feeling of loneliness that gnawed at our souls and we overcame it; that feeling I never shared with anyone, not even with Horse and Bones, or the Kid and Samuel, or Cico and Jasón.

2. "You must understand that when anybody, bruja or curandera, priest or sinner, tampers with the fate of a man that sometimes a chain of events is set into motion over which no one will have ultimate control. You must be willing to accept the responsibility."

3. I felt my body trembling as I saw the bright golden form disappear. I knew I had witnessed a miraculous thing, the appearance of a pagan god, a thing as miraculous as the curing of my Uncle Lucas. And I thought, the power of God failed where Ultima's worked; and then a sudden illumination of beauty and understanding flashed through my mind. This is what I had expected God to do at my first holy communion! If God was witness to my beholding of the golden carp then I had sinned!

Advanced Short Answer Unit Test *Bless Me, Ultima*

4. "Then maybe I do not have to be just Márez, or Luna, perhaps I can be both-" I said.

5. "I bless you in the name of all that is good and strong and beautiful, Antonio. Always have the strength to live. Love life, and if despair enters your heart, look for me in the evenings when the wind is gentle and the owls sing in the hills. I shall be with you-"

Advanced Short Answer Unit Test *Bless Me, Ultima*

IV. Vocabulary

    Listen to the vocabulary words and write them down. After you have written down all of the words, write a paragraph in which you use all the words. The paragraph must in some way relate to *Bless Me, Ultima*.

MULTIPLE CHOICE UNIT TEST 1 *Bless Me, Ultima*

I. Matching/Identification

_____ 1. Antonio Márez y Luna
_____ 2. Ultima
_____ 3. Luna family
_____ 4. Tenorio
_____ 5. Márez family
_____ 6. Narciso
_____ 7. Gabriel
_____ 8. Florence
_____ 9. Samuel
_____ 10. Cico

A. farmers, knew the secrets of the earth
B. was killed trying to warn Ultima of danger
C. believed he had no sins to confess
D. thought a lot about good vs. evil
E. told Antonio about the golden carp
F. restless, like the sea
G. wanted to move to California
H. sought revenge on Ultima
I. la curandera
J. took Antonio to see the golden carp

II. Multiple Choice

1. Which of the following towns is **not** mentioned in the novel?
    A. Guadalupe
    B. Las Pasturas
    C. El Puerto de las Lunas
    D. Gonzales

2. True or False: María wanted Antonio to become a farmer and live in Las Pasturas.
    A. True
    B. False

3. How did Antonio describe the time spent in El Puerto?
    A. He said it was hard work that he didn't like.
    B. He said he realized that he did not want to be a farmer.
    C. He said it was unpleasant because everyone fought.
    D. He said it was a happy place where people worked together.

4. What did Gabriel Márez want to do once his sons returned from the war?
    A. He wanted to buy more land and start a farm.
    B. He wanted to move to California.
    C. He wanted to go back to the llano and raise cattle.
    D. He wanted to retire and let his sons support him.

Multiple Choice Unit Test 1 *Bless Me Ultima*

5. Which of the following statements was **no**t included in Samuel's story of the carp?
    A. According to an old Indian legend, a group known as the people settled in the area, and their gods told them not to eat the carp.
    B. After a long drought and famine, they ate the carp, which angered the gods.
    C. Most of the gods wanted to turn the people into carp.
    D. One god turned into the golden carp, the protector of the waters.

6. What was the test that Tenorio made Ultima take to determine whether or not she was a witch?
    A. She had to say the rosary out loud.
    B. She had to bless herself with holy water.
    C. She had to walk through a door marked with the sign of the cross.
    D. She had to go to take holy communion.

7. True or False: When Antonio and his father were talking on the way to El Puerto, Gabriel commented that it might be time to give up the old differences between the Márez and Luna ways.
    A. True
    B. False

8. What happened at the juniper tree?
    A. Narciso killed Tenorio.
    B. Tenorio put a curse on Narciso, then went home.
    C. Tenorio killed Narciso.
    D. The sheriff got there in time and stopped the fight.

9. What did Antonio think would help him understand his dreams and questions?
    A. He thought he would understand after he made his communion.
    B. He thought he would understand if Ultima taught him.
    C. He thought he would understand when he was as old as his brothers.
    D. He thought losing his innocence would help him understand.

10. True or False: Ultima gave all of her herbs and potions to Antonio. She made him promise to continue her work and become a curandero.
    A. True
    B. False

Multiple Choice Unit Test 1 *Bless Me, Ultima*

III. Quotations Identify the speaker:

    A. Antonio   B. Ultima   C. Tenorio   D. Cico   E. Gabriel   F. Samuel

1. "-She served the people all her life, and now the people are scattered, driven like tumbleweeds by the winds of war. The war sucks everything dry, it takes the young boys overseas, and their families move to California where there is work-"

2. "We struggled against the feeling of loneliness that gnawed at our souls and we overcame it; that feeling I never shared again with anyone, not even with Horse and Bones, or the Kid and Samuel, or Cico or Jasón."

3. "You must understand that when anybody, bruja or curandera, priest or sinner, tampers with the fate of a man that sometimes a chain of events is set into motion over which no one will have ultimate control. You must be willing to accept the responsibility."

4. "¡Ay bruja!" . . . "For what you have said to shame my daughters and my good name in front of those men, I will see you dead!"

5. "It seemed that the more I knew about people the more I knew about the strange magic hidden in their hearts."

6. "I don't know, . . . except that people, grown-ups and kids, seem to want to hurt each other- and it's worse when they're in a group."

7. "I cannot tell you what to believe. Your father and mother can tell you, because you are their blood, but I cannot. As you grow into manhood you must find your own truths-"

8. "It will only end when blood is spilled. My father says that the blood of a man thickens with the desire for revenge, and if a man is to be complete again then he must let some of that thick blood flow-"

9. "You have to choose, you have to choose between the god of the church, or the beauty that is here and now-"

10. "Understanding comes with life . . . as a man grows he sees life and death, he is happy and sad, he works, plays, meets people-sometimes it takes a lifetime to acquire understanding, because in the end understanding is simply having a sympathy for people."

Multiple Choice Unit Test 1 *Bless Me, Ultima*

IV. Vocabulary Matching

1. admonished
2. clamored
3. contemptuously
4. defiance
5. emanated
6. endures
7. exasperation
8. forsaking
9. heresy
10. impending
11. interminable
12. obstacles
13. perdition
14. quavered
15. reverberating
16. scoffed
17. tenaciously
18. unperturbed
19. vigilante
20. wrought

A. dissension from dogma by a professed believer
B. endless
C. trembled
D. holding persistently to something
E. put together, created
F. anger or impatience
G. bold resistance
H. made a loud, sustained noise or outcry
I. one who takes law enforcement into one's own hands
J. reproved gently but earnestly
K. not disturbed or confused
L. came or sent forth, as from a source
M. mocked or treated with derision
N. continues in existence; lasts
O. resounding in a succession of echoes
P. disdainfully; scornfully
Q. things that oppose, or stand in the way of
R. to be about to take place
S. loss of the soul; eternal damnation
T. giving up something formerly held dear

MULTIPLE CHOICE UNIT TEST 2 *Bless Me, Ultima*

I. Matching/ Identification

_____ 1. Tenorio   A. la curandera
_____ 2. Cico   B. farmers, knew the secrets of the earth
_____ 3. Antonio Márez y Luna   C. told Antonio about the golden carp
_____ 4. Samuel   D. took Antonio to see the golden carp
_____ 5. Márez family   E. wanted to move to California
_____ 6. Florence   F. believed he had no sins to confess
_____ 7. Narciso   G. sought revenge on Ultima
_____ 8. Gabriel   H. was killed trying to warn Ultima of danger
_____ 9. Ultima   I. restless, like the sea
_____ 10. Luna family   J. thought a lot about good vs. evil

II. Multiple Choice

1. What did Antonio think would help him understand his dreams and questions?
    A. He thought he would understand after he made his communion.
    B. He thought he would understand if Ultima taught him.
    C. He thought he would understand when he was as old as his brothers.
    D. He thought losing his innocence would help him understand.

2. Why does Ultima live with the Márez family?
    A. She comes to help María, who is no longer able to care for the family.
    B. Her house in Las Pasturas burned down and she doesn't have anywhere to live.
    C. She is Antonio's godmother, and wants to make sure he is taken care of.
    D. She is getting too old to live alone, and has no one else to take care of her.

3. Antonio's brothers talked about leaving Guadalupe and going to Las Vegas or another city. What were their opinions?
    A. Eugene and Andrew wanted to move. León didn't want to leave the family.
    B. They all wanted to move.
    C. Eugene and León were in favor of the move. Andrew was concerned about their father's dream, and wasn't sure he wanted to leave the family.
    D. Only Eugene wanted to move.

Multiple Choice Unit Test 2 *Bless Me, Ultima*

4. Which of the following statements was **not** included in Samuel's story of the carp?
    A. According to an old Indian legend, a group known as the people settled in the area, and their gods told them not to eat the carp.
    B. After a long drought and famine, they ate the carp, which angered the gods.
    C. Most of the gods wanted to turn the people into carp.
    D. One god turned into the golden carp, the protector of the waters.

5. True or False: The feeling Antonio had when he saw the carp was what he had expected God to do at his first holy communion.
    A. True
    B. False

6. Why were Tenorio and the men coming to the Márez home?
    A. Tenorio wanted Ultima to cure his daughter, who was ill.
    B. Tenorio said the priest had sent him to get rid of Ultima.
    C. Tenorio's daughter wanted to become a curandera.
    D. Tenorio's daughter died. Tenorio blamed Ultima, and was coming to kill her in revenge.

7. Antonio was thinking as the family rode to El Puerto. Which of the following was **not** in his thoughts?
    A. He wondered which was more powerful-his God or the golden carp.
    B. He was wondering why God and the golden carp chose to punish people.
    C. He wondered if there could be a forgiving god.
    D. He wondered if the Virgin Mary was forgiving or punitive.

8. What was Narciso's final destination after the incident in the bar with Tenorio and why?
    A. He was going to the sheriff's office to get a warrant for Tenorio's arrest.
    B. He was going home to tend to his wounds.
    C. He was going to the church to ask for help from the priest.
    D. He was going to the Márez home to warn Ultima that Tenorio was on his way.

9. What did Antonio realize about Ultima's spirit?
    A. He realized it was the same as the presence of the river.
    B. He realized she had put it in him.
    C. He realized that it was powerful and would live forever.
    D. He realized that it was the owl.

Multiple Choice Unit Test 2 *Bless Me, Ultima*

10. What did Antonio think about the upcoming mass of the dead and burial for Ultima?
    A. He thought they proved beyond a doubt that she was not a witch.
    B. They gave him a sense of finality about her death.
    C. He thought they were just the ceremony that was required by custom.
    D. He thought it was wrong to do them, because she never said she wanted them.

Multiple Choice Unit Test 2 *Bless Me, Ultima*

III. Quotations Identify the speaker:
   A. Antonio   B. Ultima   C. Tenorio   D. Cico   E. Gabriel   F. Samuel

1. "The soul was lost, unsafe, unsure, suffering-why couldn't there be a god who would never punish his people, a god who would be forgiving all of the time?"

2. She took me to the front of the room and spoke to the other boys and girls. She pointed at me but I did not understand her. Then the other boys and girls laughed and pointed at me. I did not feel so good. Thereafter I kept away from the groups as much as I could and worked alone. I worked hard. I listened to the strange sounds. I learned new names, new words.

3. "I bless you in the name of all that is good and strong and beautiful, Antonio. Always have the strength to live. Love life, and if despair enters your heart, look for me in the evenings when the wind is gentle and the owls sing in the hills. I shall be with you-"

4. "It will only end when blood is spilled. My father says that the blood of a man thickens with the desire for revenge, and if a man is to be complete again then he must let some of that thick blood flow-"

5. "It seemed that the more I knew about people the more I knew about the strange magic hidden in their hearts."

6. "I don't know . . . except that people, grown-ups and kids, seem to want to hurt each other- and it's worse when they're in a group."

7. "-She served the people all her life, and now the people are scattered, driven like tumbleweeds by the winds of war. The war sucks everything dry . . . it takes the young boys overseas, and their families move to California where there is work-"

8. "I cannot tell you what to believe. Your father and mother can tell you, because you are their blood, but I cannot. As you grow into manhood you must find your own truths."

9. "Understanding comes with life. . . as a man grows he sees life and death, he is happy and sad, he works, plays, meets people-sometimes it takes a lifetime to acquire understanding, because in the end understanding is simply having a sympathy for people."

10. "¡Ay bruja! . . . for what you have said to shame my daughters and my good name in front of those men, I will see you dead!"

Multiple Choice Unit Test 2 *Bless Me, Ultima*

IV. Vocabulary Matching

1. abruptly
2. audacity
3. bristled
4. commotion
5. debris
6. divulged
7. emaciated
8. exuberant
9. endowed
10. exorcise
11. furrow
12. instinctively
13. intrusion
14. melee
15. resigned
16. sardonically
17. stoically
18. subsided
19. tormented
20. transfixed

A. a rut, groove, or narrow depression
B. made known something private or secret
C. scornfully or cynically mocking
D. caused to stand erect; stiffened
E. caused to undergo great pain or anguish
F. suddenly
G. rendered motionless, as with terror or amazement
H. provided with property or income
I. became less agitated or active
J. made extremely thin, especially from starvation
K. acquiescent; unresistingly accepting
L. joyous; full of high spirits
M. a violent free-for-all
N. rude or inappropriate entrance
O. to free from evil spirits or malign influences
P. rubble or wreckage
Q. an agitated disturbance
R. fearlessness; boldness
S. done by innate aptitude
T. unaffected by pain or pleasure

ANSWER SHEET   Multiple Choice Unit Tests *Bless Me, Ultima*

I. Matching

1. ____
2. ____
3. ____
4. ____
5. ____
6. ____
7. ____
8. ____
9. ____
10. ____

II. Multiple Choice

1. (A) (B) (C) (D)
2. (A) (B) (C) (D)
3. (A) (B) (C) (D)
4. (A) (B) (C) (D)
5. (A) (B) (C) (D)
6. (A) (B) (C) (D)
7. (A) (B) (C) (D)
8. (A) (B) (C) (D)
9. (A) (B) (C) (D)
10. (A) (B) (C) (D)

III. Quotations

1. ____
2. ____
3. ____
4. ____
5. ____
6. ____
7. ____
8. ____
9. ____
10. ____

IV. Vocabulary

1. ____
2. ____
3. ____
4. ____
5. ____
6. ____
7. ____
8. ____
9. ____
10. ____
11. ____
12. ____
13. ____
14. ____
15. ____
16. ____
17. ____
18. ____
19. ____
20. ____

ANSWER SHEET KEY   Multiple Choice Unit Test 1 *Bless Me, Ultima*

<table>
<tr><td colspan="2">I. Matching</td><td colspan="2">III. Quotations</td><td colspan="2">IV. Vocabulary</td></tr>
<tr><td>1.</td><td>D</td><td>1.</td><td>E</td><td>1.</td><td>J</td></tr>
<tr><td>2.</td><td>I</td><td>2.</td><td>A</td><td>2.</td><td>H</td></tr>
<tr><td>3.</td><td>A</td><td>3.</td><td>B</td><td>3.</td><td>P</td></tr>
<tr><td>4.</td><td>H</td><td>4.</td><td>C</td><td>4.</td><td>G</td></tr>
<tr><td>5.</td><td>F</td><td>5.</td><td>A</td><td>5.</td><td>L</td></tr>
<tr><td>6.</td><td>B</td><td>6.</td><td>F</td><td>6.</td><td>N</td></tr>
<tr><td>7.</td><td>G</td><td>7.</td><td>B</td><td>7.</td><td>F</td></tr>
<tr><td>8.</td><td>C</td><td>8.</td><td>F</td><td>8.</td><td>T</td></tr>
<tr><td>9.</td><td>E</td><td>9.</td><td>D</td><td>9.</td><td>A</td></tr>
<tr><td>10.</td><td>J</td><td>10.</td><td>E</td><td>10.</td><td>R</td></tr>
<tr><td></td><td></td><td></td><td></td><td>11.</td><td>B</td></tr>
<tr><td></td><td></td><td></td><td></td><td>12.</td><td>Q</td></tr>
<tr><td></td><td></td><td></td><td></td><td>13.</td><td>S</td></tr>
<tr><td></td><td></td><td></td><td></td><td>14.</td><td>C</td></tr>
<tr><td></td><td></td><td></td><td></td><td>15.</td><td>O</td></tr>
<tr><td></td><td></td><td></td><td></td><td>16.</td><td>M</td></tr>
<tr><td></td><td></td><td></td><td></td><td>17.</td><td>D</td></tr>
<tr><td></td><td></td><td></td><td></td><td>18.</td><td>K</td></tr>
<tr><td></td><td></td><td></td><td></td><td>19.</td><td>I</td></tr>
<tr><td></td><td></td><td></td><td></td><td>20.</td><td>E</td></tr>
</table>

II. Multiple Choice

1. (A) (B) (C) ( )
2. (A) ( ) (C) (D)
3. (A) (B) (C) ( )
4. (A) ( ) (C) (D)
5. (A) (B) ( ) (D)
6. (A) (B) ( ) (D)
7. ( ) (B) (C) (D)
8. (A) (B) ( ) (D)
9. ( ) (B) (C) (D)
10. (A) ( ) (C) (D)

ANSWER SHEET KEY Multiple Choice Unit Test 2 *Bless Me, Ultima*

<table>
<tr><td colspan="2">I. Matching</td><td colspan="2">III. Quotations</td><td colspan="2">IV. Vocabulary</td></tr>
<tr><td>1.</td><td>G</td><td>1.</td><td>A</td><td>1.</td><td>F</td></tr>
<tr><td>2.</td><td>D</td><td>2.</td><td>A</td><td>2.</td><td>R</td></tr>
<tr><td>3.</td><td>J</td><td>3.</td><td>B</td><td>3.</td><td>D</td></tr>
<tr><td>4.</td><td>C</td><td>4.</td><td>F</td><td>4.</td><td>Q</td></tr>
<tr><td>5.</td><td>I</td><td>5.</td><td>A</td><td>5.</td><td>P</td></tr>
<tr><td>6.</td><td>F</td><td>6.</td><td>F</td><td>6.</td><td>B</td></tr>
<tr><td>7.</td><td>H</td><td>7.</td><td>E</td><td>7.</td><td>J</td></tr>
<tr><td>8.</td><td>E</td><td>8.</td><td>B</td><td>8.</td><td>L</td></tr>
<tr><td>9.</td><td>A</td><td>9.</td><td>E</td><td>9.</td><td>H</td></tr>
<tr><td>10.</td><td>B</td><td>10.</td><td>C</td><td>10.</td><td>O</td></tr>
</table>

II. Multiple Choice

1. ( ) (B) (C) (D)
2. (A) (B) (C) ( )
3. (A) (B) ( ) (D)
4. (A) (B) ( ) (D)
5. ( ) (B) (C) (D)
6. (A) (B) (C) ( )
7. ( ) (B) (C) (D)
8. (A) (B) (C) ( )
9. (A) (B) (C) ( )
10. (A) (B) ( ) (D)

11. A
12. S
13. N
14. M
15. K
16. C
17. T
18. I
19. E
20. G

UNIT RESOURCE MATERIALS

BULLETIN BOARD IDEAS *Bless Me, Ultima*

1. Save one corner of the board for the best of students' *Bless Me, Ultima* writing assignments. You may want to use background maps of New Mexico to represent the setting of the novel.

2. Take one of the word search puzzles from the extra activities packet and with a marker copy it over in a large size on the bulletin board. Write the clue words to find to one side. Invite students prior to and after class to find the words and circle them on the bulletin board.

3. Have students find or draw pictures that they think resemble the people in the book.

4. Invite students to help make an interactive bulletin board quiz. Give each student a half-sheet of paper (about 4"x5') folded in half so that it can open. On the outside flap, have each student write a description of one of the characters in the text. On the inside, they will write the name of the character. You can staple or tack these papers to the bulletin board so that the students can read the descriptions and lift the flaps to find the answers.

5. Collect pictures of the cities mentioned in the book.

6. Make a display of common classroom items. Write their names in English and Spanish.

7. Make a display of travel posters of New Mexico, the southwestern United States, and Mexico.

8. Display articles about Rudolfo Anaya and critiques of his work.

9. Have students design postcards depicting the settings of the book.

10. Make collages of the people and events from the book.

EXTRA ACTIVITIES *Bless Me, Ultima*

One of the difficulties in teaching a novel is that all students don't read at the same speed. One student who likes to read may take the book home and finish it in a day or two. Sometimes a few students finish the in-class assignments early. The problem, then, is finding suitable extra activities for students.

One thing that helps is to keep a little library in the classroom. For this unit on *Bless Me, Ultima*, you might check out from the school or public library other books by Rudolfo Anaya. There are also many other novels by Mexican-American writers that students may enjoy reading.

Other things you may keep on hand are word search puzzles. Several puzzles relating directly to *Bless Me, Ultima* are included in the unit. Feel free to duplicate them.

Some students may like to draw. You might devise a contest or allow some extra-credit grade for students who draw characters or scenes from *Bless Me, Ultima.* Note, too, that if the students do not want to keep their drawings you may pick up some extra bulletin board materials this way. If you have a contest and you supply the prize. You could, possibly, make the drawing itself a non-refundable entry fee.

Have maps, a globe, and travel brochures on hand for easy reference. Travel agencies and automobile clubs are good sources for these materials.

The pages which follow contain games, puzzles, and worksheets. The keys, when appropriate, immediately follow the puzzle or worksheet. There are two main groups of activities: one group for the unit; that is, generally relating to the Bless *Me, Ultima* text, and another group of activities related strictly to the *Bless Me, Ultima* vocabulary.

Directions for the games, puzzles, and worksheets are self-explanatory. The object here is to provide you with extra materials you may use in any way you choose.

Have students write to the author, giving their impressions of the book, and asking any questions they have. If you choose to send the letters, the publisher's address is in the front of the book.

MORE ACTIVITIES *Bless Me, Ultima*

1. Pick one of the incidents for students to dramatize. Encourage students to write dialog for the characters. (Perhaps you could assign various stories to different groups of students so more than one story could be acted and more students could participate.)

2. Have students design a book cover (front and back and inside flaps) for *Bless Me, Ultima.*

3. Have students design a bulletin board (ready to be put up; not just sketched) for *Bless Me, Ultima.*

4. Make a class newspaper based on the events in *Bless Me, Ultima.* Individuals or groups can choose an event, then write a headline and short article.

5. Use some of the related topics (noted earlier for an in-class library) as topics for research, reports, written papers, or as topics for guest speakers.

6. Help students design and produce a talk show. Choose one of the story incidents as the topic. The host will interview the various characters. (Students should make up the questions they want the host to ask the characters.)

7. Have students work in pairs to create an interview with one of the characters. One student should be the interviewer and the other should be the interviewee. Students can work together to compose questions for the interviewer to ask. Each pair of students could present their interview to the class.

8. Invite students who have read other books by Rudolfo Anaya to present book talks to the class.

9. Invite students who have read a biography of Rudolfo Anaya to tell the class about his life.

10. Invite someone who has lived in one of the areas mentioned in the book to speak to the class.

11. Have students hold small group discussions related to topics in the book. Assign a recorder and a speaker for each group. Have the speaker from each group make a report to the class.

12. Speak to the students in a different language for a while so they can understand how Antonio must have felt his first day in school. Then hold a discussion about your students' feelings when they didn't understand you.

WORD SEARCH *Bless Me, Ultima*

```
Y S T G L T V Q R V A G K Y A P J X I S D O M D P D S R E P I N U J
W C N D I K J M N D F C I D Q B L Q D A Y P Y F O C O X Q F M S O T
C R O S S R S Z Q L E L V C I Y E O U C X N K J L U E D C W R D L W
G L E D N A R G A L G B O Q E G Q L J U S Z T V N N W M W F V F L M
R M H E M E A J I E T K O R M N R O E L B Z A F V X S Q R V K M Z Z
I D T U M N A E N V M V O R E H B C L A K Z O D U X O T Y P E F V M
Y I E F T S L G B B L D N D A N W I K E N K Y Q B D P U R E T A W B
I L U O E P L A M O B I T W B H C C X V Y G D E H Q V M I N E E E Z
B R N R U V O Y N B Q A L T P M V E E U M E K E C H H L T I W B S E
L I E E A Z W I X S D O Z R L O N L I N E S S T L J Y C Q E T Y C L
O H R O J Y T F E I J U W N N J V I K S H Q V G Z S O X P K Y T Q L
T T O W S N A E V S A M A L H O P T S E P Y U K U V U G D K K E R E
O Z B L E N V N X H T L I B Z I H L W M Z W J S Y T K C A F X U K T
W L Z M H T I S A Y O Q T E E V A C Q F W W Y Q O N F G Q B P G Z T
Q I E T E J P E C X G F R Z R R O S A T S E A M S S I M I L R Z X E
E R T D K Z C E E B U B S W A J A Q F P L C L U P Y G O G F U I M B
T O E C H W B N V O T T W E M E N M O Q I G V F T P H J Y G J N E J
J C R H H F Q O I R S Z V G I V V I I G M K T J I G E T Q L A G A L
Y G D M U E G H O D Z S D F R S T R M T W Q D Z H J Z J X S W G U C
C E A H M C U S M F T H F Q A G O F T Y L O T X T B H G B T V Y O F
L Z F G J B H O J A Q H Y I W U M R F H D U M C Q X I I O J G O T F
S Y U D V F E X I X T C E J J Q O M M I E Y U P A Z K A E Z X E P W
J M L M Y P E H B X C W Y I Y B V O Y D D K N K I M Q L B Y Y I F X
```

LAGRANDE	LUNA	WATER
FLORENCE	MAREZ	TREMENTINO
SAMUEL	EL PUERTO	JUNIPER
CICO	ULTIMA	EYE
ABEL	OWL	TELLEZ
DEBORAH	ROSIES	LUCAS
THERESA	MISS MAESTAS	CROSS
ANTONIO	LONLINESS	ANAYA
GABRIEL	WAR	WITCH

CROSSWORD *Bless Me, Ultima*

CROSSWORD CLUES *Bless Me, Ultima*

ACROSS

3 Well-mannered Marez daughter
5 Author
6 His Indian told the story about the carp
8 Where Marez boys were at the beginning of the novel
11 What surrounded the town of Guadalupe
12 Antonio expected to get answers from God after making it
14 Luna uncle cured by Ultima
17 Ultima's home before coming to the Marez home: Las ___
20 Luna uncle who drove to warn Ultima
23 Gabriel's preferred occupation
25 Farming family
26 What owl took from Tenorio
29 Coached in manners by her sister
30 Wanted revenge for his brother's murder
31 Color of the god-carp
33 Always running: ___ Kid
34 Town where Marez family lived
35 What Antonio felt his first day at school

DOWN

1 Died trying to warn Ultima of danger
2 Told Antonio the story of the carp
3 How Florence died
4 In conflict about his destiny
6 Tree where Narciso died
7 Ultima's pet and spirit
9 Tenorio's family name
10 Took Antonio to see the golden carp
13 First grade teacher: Miss ___
15 What the people were turned into
16 What a witch couldn't stand to wear
18 Believed his house was cursed
19 Antonio's native language
21 Ultima's occupation
22 Home of Maria's farming relatives: El ___ De La Luna
24 Wanted revenge for his daughters' deaths
25 War-crazed murderer
27 Ultima was accused of being one
28 Believed he had never sinned
31 Term of respect for Ultima: La ___
32 Most forceful brother

CROSSWORD ANSWER KEY *Bless Me, Ultima*

MATCHING WORKSHEET 1 Bless Me, Ultima

Directions: Place the letter of the matching description on the blank line.

____ 1.	Antonio	A.	what "the people" were turned into
____ 2.	Narciso	B.	used as the witch test for Ultima
____ 3.	carp	C.	his Indian told the story about the carp
____ 4.	owl	D.	feeling Antonio had his first day at school
____ 5.	El Puerto de la Luna	E.	Antonio expected to get answers after he made it
____ 6.	communion	F.	wanted revenge for his daughters' deaths
____ 7.	Eugene	G.	took Antonio to see the golden carp
____ 8.	cross	H.	always running
____ 9.	Deborah	I.	in conflict about his destiny
____ 10.	Vitamin Kid	J.	war-crazed sheriff killer
____ 11.	Luna	K.	mannerly Márez daughter
____ 12.	juniper tree	L.	town where farming uncles lived
____ 13.	Tenorio	M.	method of Florence's death
____ 14.	Jasón	N.	family had not had a priest for several generations
____ 15.	eye	O.	Antonio's native language
____ 16.	Spanish	P.	most forceful brother
____ 17.	drowned	Q.	died trying to warn Ultima of danger
____ 18.	Lupito	R.	what the owl took from Tenorio
____ 19.	Cico	S.	Ultima's pet and spirit
____ 20.	loneliness	T.	where Narciso was shot

ANSWER KEY MATCHING WORKSHEET 1 *Bless Me, Ultima*
Directions: Place the letter of the matching description on the blank line.

I	1.	Antonio	A.	what "the people" were turned into
Q	2.	Narciso	B.	used as the witch test for Ultima
A	3.	carp	C.	his Indian told the story about the carp
S	4.	owl	D.	feeling Antonio had his first day at school
L	5.	El Puerto de la Luna	E.	Antonio expected to get answers after he made it
E	6.	communion	F.	wanted revenge for his daughters' deaths
P	7.	Eugene	G.	took Antonio to see the golden carp
B	8.	cross	H.	always running
K	9.	Deborah	I.	in conflict about his destiny
H	10.	Vitamin Kid	J.	war-crazed sheriff killer
N	11.	Luna	K.	mannerly Márez daughter
T	12.	juniper tree	L.	town where farming uncles lived
F	13.	Tenorio	M.	method of Florence's death
C	14.	Jasón	N.	family had not had a priest for several generations
R	15.	eye	O.	Antonio's native language
O	16.	Spanish	P.	most forceful brother
M	17.	drowned	Q.	died trying to warn Ultima of danger
J	18.	Lupito	R.	what the owl took from Tenorio
G	19.	Cico	S.	Ultima's pet and spirit
D	20.	loneliness	T.	where Narciso was shot

MATCHING WORKSHEET 2 *Bless Me, Ultima*

Directions: Place the letter of the matching definition on the blank line.

____ 1.	Tellez	A.	tried unsuccessfully to get Andrew's help
____ 2.	witch	B.	what surrounded the town
____ 3.	Anaya	C.	wanted revenge for his brother's murder
____ 4.	Florence	D.	said he had no sins
____ 5.	Pedro	E.	Gabriel's preferred occupation
____ 6.	las Pasturas	F.	restless sea-blood family
____ 7.	water	G.	author
____ 8.	golden	H.	Ultima's home before living with Márez family
____ 9.	Theresa	I.	Luna uncle who drove to warn Ultima
____ 10.	la Grande	J.	Ultima's occupation
____ 11.	Chávez	K.	thought his house was cursed
____ 12.	Samuel	L.	coached on manners by her sister
____ 13.	Trementina	M.	first grade teacher
____ 14.	Narciso	N.	town where Márez family lived
____ 15.	Guadalupe	O.	what Ultima was accused of being
____ 16.	Maestas	P.	told Antonio about the carp
____ 17.	Márez	Q.	term of respect for Ultima
____ 18.	vaquero	R.	color of the god-carp
____ 19.	curandera	S.	Tenorio's family name
____ 20.	Lucas	T.	Luna uncle saved by Ultima

ANSWER KEY RESOURCE MATCHING QUIZ 2 *Bless Me, Ultima*
Directions: Place the letter of the matching definition on the blank line.

K	1.	Tellez	A.	tried unsuccessfully to get Andrew's help
O	2.	witch	B.	what surrounded the town
G	3.	Anaya	C.	wanted revenge for his brother's murder
D	4.	Florence	D.	said he had no sins
I	5.	Pedro	E.	Gabriel's preferred occupation
H	6.	las Pasturas	F.	restless sea-blood family
B	7.	water	G.	author
R	8.	golden	H.	Ultima's home before living with Márez family
L	9.	Theresa	I.	Luna uncle who drove to warn Ultima
Q	10.	la Grande	J.	Ultima's occupation
C	11.	Chávez	K.	thought his house was cursed
P	12.	Samuel	L.	coached on manners by her sister
S	13.	Trementina	M.	first grade teacher
A	14.	Narciso	N.	town where Márez family lived
N	15.	Guadalupe	O.	what Ultima was accused of being
M	16.	Maestas	P.	told Antonio about the carp
F	17.	Márez	Q.	term of respect for Ultima
E	18.	vaquero	R.	color of the god-carp
J	19.	curandera	S.	Tenorio's family name
T	20.	Lucas	T.	Luna uncle saved by Ultima

JUGGLE WORD GAME *Bless Me, Ultima*

SCRAMBLED	WORD	CLUE
yaAna	Anaya	author
onntioA	Antonio	in conflict about his destiny
parc	Carp	what "the people" were turned into
heÁzvC	Chávez	wanted revenge for his brother's murder
Coic	Cico	took Antonio to see the golden carp
momounicn	Communion	Antonio expected to get answers from God after making it
rcsos	Cross	what a witch couldn't stand to be near
ruacnerad	Curandera	Ultima's occupation
broaDeh	Deborah	well-mannered Márez daughter
dnreodw	Drowned	how Florence died
lEPtutroe	El Puerto	home of María's farming relatives
Euegen	Eugene	most forceful brother
yee	Eye	what owl took from Tenorio
lrocreFne	Florence	believed he had never sinned
gledon	Golden	color of the god-carp
daalGuupe	Guadalupe	town where Márez family lived
Jósan	Jasón	his Indian told the story about the carp
juniper	Juniper	tree where Narciso died
raGanled	La Grande	term of respect for Ultima
rlasPatuass	Las Pasturas	Ultima's home before coming to Márez home
lssoneliesse	Loneliness	what Antonio felt his first day at school
Lcusa	Lucas	Luna uncle cured by Ultima
nuaL	Luna	farming family
tupLio	Lupito	war-crazed murderer
saMseat	Maestas	first grade teaacher
záerM	Márez	family with restless sea-blood
aircsNo	Narciso	died trying to warn Ultima of danger
lwo	Owl	Ultima's pet and spirit
Preod	Pedro	Luna uncle who drove to warn Ultima
uSaelm	Samuel	told Antonio the story of the carp
aSnspih	Spanish	Antonio's native language
TleezL	Tellez	believed his house was cursed
TorionE	Tenorio	wanted revenge for his daughters' deaths
Theesar	Theresa	coached in manners by her sister
Trainnemet	Trementina	Tenorio's family name
evaqrou	Vaquero	Gabriel's preferred occupation
minKaidtVi	Vitamin Kid	always running
raw	War	where Márez boys were at beginning of novel

VOCABULARY RESOURCE MATERIALS

VOCABULARY WORD SEARCH *Bless Me, Ultima*

All the words in this list are associated with *Bless Me, Ultima* with emphasis on the vocabulary words being studied in the unit. The words are placed backwards, forward, diagonally, up and down.

```
Q G I W B X P D M M T F R A P H A O A L I K F W L R E I S M E W F C D
E S Q G P F Z L C S D D W C U X X T B N D T P R H S L G E V X N B V F
S M K Z O G Z T G A D I K V Z L R F T I Y Q E O L K P G Z E Q D S T A
D Z A B H O N U D K R H C G T H S E A F P U A U U I Q L T W Z O T U S
N C J C S X T I N N J M G A S Z R A L X F H B G D R G A Q O J Z U X N
X Z I U I V K C K S L K N P E M Y L B A K H R H I T A G H U B I A E D
Y O C B D A S M D A Q K T D I N A S E T O M U T D P D P M X J V O X H
Q Y L L E O T C Z O S N I N C Z C R O P T N P T A S M W L C V C F Y N
N C A Z J A Y E U N O R A J W V P X H V Y F T O I T O Y T H S L W T O
J V M O Q N W U D I H B O K Y P P S T Q S C L Y D R N Y C T N Y J B F
S P O K K Q A F T Y L K D F O L E L W X H L Y C R J I H J S R F G W T
C U R U M J R A T E Y W E N R O X T P D T Q K U L Q S Y G R F T N O E
K S E Z L Q R V G K R Z T O K E K E A A A D F J B Q H J V H N Z A S T
Q E D A W E D O P L Y I A I S N J R T D E F I A N C E G U E S E Y B K
F F W E P Q K K B C A J L T K Z J V Z X H N H D Z L D G L J I I M M L
A W R S C T O Q Q Z U D U I I H N W I P S S D L S Z L U U I D E K V O
Z W A Z M W G P L Q Q F P D D I H F F W X Y K O Z F C J Z F F K N W C
N X Y F V O S C B Q P E I R A B S O I F Z D N X W C E T N A L I G I V
E Y J L F K I Q B E M U N E F N A U A A U G I X U E N G I W B Y Y E M
N O I T U L O S E R R F A P A J C H B Z S R K S S Z D A A E T H W Z O
H I Y Z S S Z F H I N S M R M D P I C N O I T O M M O C F E M U B S K
F A C W Z R Y J V T S W T S T U P O R F D G N I T E E L F K V B E I V
C W I D C K W G X F W Z W A R P A M W S D N O B A G A V U U X I N V H
```

ABRUPTLY	FLEETING	SHEATHS
ADMONISHED	FORSAKING	STUPOR
CLAMORED	FURROW	SUCCULENT
COMMOTION	INTERMINABLE	TRANSFIXED
DEFIANCE	MANIPULATED	VAGABONDS
EMACIATED	MOTES	VIGILANTE
ENDOWED	PERDITION	WROUGHT
EXASPERATION	RESOLUTION	

VOCABULARY CROSSWORD *Bless Me, Ultima*

VOCABULARY CROSSWORD CLUES *Bless Me, Ultima*

ACROSS
2 Cases for sword or knife blades
5 Lying in wait, as in ambush
6 Full of juice or sap; juicy
8 Those who take law enforcement upon themselves
10 Firm determination
12 Wander in search of food or provisions
13 Violent free-for-all
16 Imperfection that mars or impairs
17 Violated the sacredness of; profaned
19 Unpleasantly sharp, pungent, or bitter to smell
20 Moving swiftly; rapid or nimble
21 Bold resistance
24 Continuous, low, dull humming sound
25 Caused to stand erect; stiffened
28 Fearlessness; boldness
29 About to take place
30 Sung softly or in a humming way
31 Made known something private or secret

DOWN
1 Trembled
3 Dissension from dogma by a professed believer
4 State of mental numbness, a daze
6 Mocked or treated for derision
7 Endless
9 Morally, socially, or legally obliged to another; beholden
11 Free from evil spirits or malign influences
14 Ghosts or apparitions
15 Influenced or managed shrewdly or deviously
18 Pride; joy
20 A rut, groove, or narrow depression
21 Rubble or wreckage
22 Continues in existence; lasts
23 Rude or inappropriate entrance
26 Became less agitated or active
27 Cut into the surface of

VOCABULARY CROSSWORD ANSWER KEY *Bless Me, Ultima*

VOCABULARY WORKSHEET 1 *Bless Me, Ultima*

_____ 1. unpleasantly sharp, pungent, or bitter to smell
   A. emaciated   B. acrid   C. exuberant   D. impending

_____ 2. making claims to unwarranted importance
   A. succulent   B. forsaking   C. arrogant   D. indebted

_____ 3. an imperfection that mars or impairs
   A. blemish   B. melee   C. stupor   D. debris

_____ 4. a company of travelers journeying together
   A. commotion   B. caravan   C. furrow   D. motes

_____ 5. offered in response
   A. pulsating   B. subsided   C. impending   D. countered

_____ 6. bold resistance
   A. defiance   B. forsaking   C. manipulated   D. desecrated

_____ 7. made known (something private or secret)
   A. admonished   B. emaciated   C. divulged   D. etched

_____ 8. came forth, as from a source
   A. bristled   B. crooned   C. endowed   D. emanated

_____ 9. continues in existence; lasts
   A. interminable B. endures   C. pulsating   D. stupor

_____ 10. cut into the surface of
   A. etched   B. furrow   C. reverberating D. scoffed

_____ 11. to free from evil spirits
   A. heresy   B. tormented   C. exorcise   D. wrought

_____ 12. to be about to take place
   A. abruptly   B. impending   C. contemptuously D. forsaking

_____ 13. things that oppose, or stand in the way of
   A. heresy   B. incantation C. sheaths   D. obstacles

_____ 14. trembled
   A. quavered   B. subsided   C. illuminated   D. admonished

_____ 15. scornfully or cynically mocking
   A. emphatically B. contemptuously C. sardonically D. instinctively

_____ 16. mocked or treated with derision
   A. dysentery   B. forage   C. scoffed   D. indebted

_____ 17. unaffected by pleasure or pain
   A. resigned   B. stoically   C. tenaciously   D. tormented

_____ 18. became less agitated or active
   A. unperturbed   B. resolution   C. resigned   D. subsided

_____ 19. rendered motionless, as with terror, or amazement
   A. transfixed   B. stupor   C. perdition   D. quavered

_____ 20. one who takes law enforcement into one's own hands
   A. phantoms   B. caravan   C. drone   D. vigilante

ANSWER KEY VOCABULARY WORKSHEET 1 *Bless Me, Ultima*

B 1. unpleasantly sharp, pungent, or bitter to smell
   A. emaciated **B. acrid** C. exuberant D. impending

C 2. making claims to unwarranted importance
   A. succulent B. forsaking **C. arrogant** D. indebted

A 3. an imperfection that mars or impairs
   A. blemish B. melee C. stupor D. debris

B 4. a company of travelers journeying together
   A. commotion **B. caravan** C. furrow D. motes

D 5. offered in response
   A. pulsating B. subsided C. impending **D. countered**

A 6. bold resistance
   A. defiance B. forsaking C. manipulated D. elation

C 7. made known (something private or secret)
   A. admonished B. emaciated **C. divulged** D. etched

D 8. came forth, as from a source
   A. bristled B. crooned C. endowed **D. emanated**

B 9. continues in existence; lasts
   A. interminable **B. endures** C. pulsating D. stupor

A 10. cut into the surface of
   A. etched B. furrow C. reverberating D. scoffed

C 11. to free from evil spirits
   A. heresy B. tormented **C. exorcise** D. wrought

B 12. to be about to take place
   A. abruptly **B. impending** C. contemptuously D. forsaking

D 13. things that oppose, or stand in the way of
   A. heresy B. incantation C. sheaths **D. obstacles**

A 14. trembled
   A. quavered B. subsided C. illuminated D. admonished

C 15. scornfully or cynically mocking
   A. emphatically B. contemptuously **C. sardonically** D. instinctively

C 16. mocked or treated with derision
   A. dysentery B. forage **C. scoffed** D. indebted

B 17. unaffected by pleasure or pain
   A. resigned **B. stoically** C. tenaciously D. tormented

D 18. became less agitated or active
   A. unperturbed B. resolution C. resigned **D. subsided**

A 19. rendered motionless, as with terror, or amazement
   A. transfixed B. stupor C. perdition D. quavered

D 20. one who takes law enforcement into one's own hands
   A. phantoms B. caravan C. drone **D. vigilante**

VOCABULARY WORKSHEET 2 *Bless Me, Ultima*

Directions: Place the letter of the matching definition on the blank line.

_____	1. audacity	A.	dissension from dogma by a professed believer
_____	2. bristled	B.	disdainfully; scornfully
_____	3. commotion	C.	resounding in a succession of echoes
_____	4. contemptuously	D.	caused to stand erect; stiffened
_____	5. debris	E.	put together, created
_____	6. emaciated	F.	acquiescent; unresistingly accepting
_____	7. endowed	G.	done by innate aptitude
_____	8. exasperation	H.	rubble or wreckage
_____	9. forsaking	I.	an agitated disturbance
_____	10. heresy	J.	fearlessness, boldness
_____	11. instinctively	K.	giving up something formerly held dear
_____	12. intrusion	L.	loss of the soul; eternal damnation
_____	13. melee	M.	not disturbed or confused
_____	14. obstacles	N.	made extremely thin
_____	15. perdition	O.	holding persistently to something
_____	16. resigned	P.	anger or impatience
_____	17. reverberating	Q.	things that oppose, or stand in the way of
_____	18. tenaciously	R.	rude or inappropriate entrance
_____	19. unperturbed	S.	provided with property or income
_____	20. wrought	T.	a violent free-for-all

ANSWER KEY VOCABULARY WORKSHEET 2 *Bless Me, Ultima*

Directions: Place the letter of the matching definition on the blank line.

J	1. audacity		A.	dissension from dogma by a professed believer
D	2. bristled		B.	disdainfully; scornfully
I	3. commotion		C.	resounding in a succession of echoes
B	4. contemptuously		D.	caused to stand erect; stiffened
H	5. debris		E.	put together, created
N	6. emaciated		F.	acquiescent; unresistingly accepting
S	7. endowed		G.	done by innate aptitude
P	8. exasperation		H.	rubble or wreckage
K	9. forsaking		I.	an agitated disturbance
A	10. heresy		J.	fearlessness, boldness
G	11. instinctively		K.	giving up something formerly held dear
R	12. intrusion		L.	loss of the soul; eternal damnation
T	13. melee		M.	not disturbed or confused
Q	14. obstacles		N.	made extremely thin
L	15. perdition		O.	holding persistently to something
F	16. resigned		P.	anger or impatience
C	17. reverberating		Q.	things that oppose, or stand in the way of
O	18. tenaciously		R.	rude or inappropriate entrance
M	19. unperturbed		S.	provided with property or income
E	20. wrought		T.	a violent free-for-all

VOCABULARY JUGGLE LETTER REVIEW GAME *Bless Me, Ultima*

SCRAMBLED	WORD	CLUE
LABTYURP	ABRUPTLY	suddenly
AIRCD	ACRID	unpleasantly sharp, pungent, or bitter to smell
MADONDSIEH	ADMONISHED	reproved gently but earnestly
ATRGROAN	ARROGANT	making claims to unwarranted importance
IUCDACAYT	AUDACITY	fearlessness; boldness
EBILSMH	BLEMISH	an imperfection that mars or impairs
TDBSRILE	BRISTLED	caused to stand erect; stiffened
AVCRANA	CARAVAN	a company of travelers journeying together
MOCLREAD	CLAMORED	made a loud, sustained noise or outcry
TCOOMINOM	COMMOTION	an agitated disturbance
SMUCOYUNTTEPOL	CONTEMPTUOUSLY	disdainfully; scornfully
CROUTEEDN	COUNTERED	offered in response
NOCOEDR	CROONED	sung softly or in a humming way
EDRIBS	DEBRIS	rubble or wreckage
ADEFINEC	DEFIANCE	bold resistance
CREATEDSED	DESECRATED	violated the sacredness of; profaned
UEDISITUDEQ	DISQUIETUDE	worried unease; anxiety
GLUEDIVD	DIVULGED	made known (something private or secret)
ONERD	DRONE	a continuous low dull humming sound
NDSETEYYR	DYSENTERY	inflammatory disorder of the lower intestinal tract
OLATINE	ELATION	pride; joy
DIMEACATE	EMACIATED	made extremely thin, especially from starvation
MATEENDA	EMANATED	to come or send forth, as from a source
MEPAYTCAHLIL	EMPHATICALLY	positively; definitely
DENODEW	ENDOWED	provided with property or income
RUDENES	ENDURES	continues in existence; lasts
THEDEC	ETCHED	cut into the surface of
ATEXASPNOREI	EXASPERATION	anger or impatience
XUETRANBE	EXUBERANT	joyous; full of high spirits
CEROXCIES	EXORCISE	to free from evil spirits or malign influences
NFETIEGL	FLEETING	moving swiftly; rapid or nimble

VOCABULARY REVIEW GAME *Bless Me, Ultima*

SCRAMBLED	WORD	CLUE
ARGFEO	FORAGE	to wander in search of food or provisions
OSAKFINGR	FORSAKING	giving up something formerly held dear
RFOURW	FURROW	a rut, groove, or narrow depression
SHEREY	HERESY	dissension from dogma by a professed believer
MILDALTUINE	ILLUMINATED	lit up
GNEPMIDIN	IMPENDING	to be about to take place
NNAIIATNOTC	INCANTATION	ritual recitation of spells to produce a magic effect
BEEITDDN	INDEBTED	morally, socially, or legally obligated to another
ITCSEIVLNNTYI	INSTINCTIVELY	done by innate aptitude
BITEAREMINLN	INTERMINABLE	endless
RSNTIOUNI	INTRUSION	rude or inappropriate entrance
OLEIRVRCEBA	IRREVOCABLE	impossible to retract or withdraw
UINLKGR	LURKING	lying in wait, as in ambush
TMELDAPUINA	MANIPULATED	influenced or managed shrewdly or deviously
EELEME	MELEE	a violent free-for-all
TOMES	MOTES	very small particles; specks
TOSCLEBAS	OBSTACLES	things that oppose, or stand in the way of
ORDNIEIPT	PERDITION	loss of the soul; eternal damnation
AOMSPNTH	PHANTOMS	ghosts or an apparitions
SPUNLAIGT	PULSATING	expanding and contracting rhythmically; beating
VEUDRQEA	QUAVERED	trembled
ISENEDGR	RESIGNED	acquiescent; unresistingly accepting
UONOTISLRE	RESOLUTION	firm determination
TEEIRAGRVBREN	REVERBERATING	resounding in a succession of echoes
DNIALARYLSOC	SARDONICALLY	scornfully or cynically mocking
FFCSEDO	SCOFFED	mocked or treated with derision
HSSTHEA	SHEATHS	cases for sword or knife blades
ILCOYTSLA	STOICALLY	unaffected by pleasure or pain; impassive

VOCABULARY REVIEW GAME *Bless Me, Ultima*

SCRAMBLED	WORD	CLUE
TROSUP	STUPOR	a state of mental numbness from shock; a daze
IDDUSSBE	SUBSIDED	became less agitated or active
CSNLETUUC	SUCCULENT	full of juice or sap; juicy
NOLCTUEAIYS	TENACIOUSLY	holding persistently to something
OTENEDRMT	TORMENTED	caused to undergo great pain or anguish
SIXANREDFT	TRANSFIXED	rendered motionless, as with terror, or amazement
DUNREUETPRB	UNPERTURBED	not disturbed or confused
DOGASVANB	VAGABONDS	homeless people who move from place to place
SENTGIVIAL	VIGILANTES	those who take law enforcement upon themselves
UOHTRGW	WROUGHT	put together; created

www.ingramcontent.com/pod-product-compliance
Lightning Source LLC
Chambersburg PA
CBHW051409070526
44584CB00023B/3353